R
PSALMS
in 30 Days
with
CANTICLES
&
SAYINGS of JESUS

meditation rendering by
Stephen Joseph Wolf

www.idjc.org

*Rainbow Psalms in 30 Days
with Canticles & Sayings of Jesus*
Copyright © 2023
Stephen Joseph Wolf

All rights reserved. No part of this book may be copied or reproduced in any form or by any means, except for the inclusion of brief quotations in a review or the songs understood by the publisher to be in the public domain, without written permission of the publisher.

This arrangement follows closely the 30 day cycle for Morning and Evening as found in the ecumenical *Book of Common Prayer*:

ISBN 978-1-937081-79-9

ISBN 978-1-937081-72-0 *Dawn & Dusk Rainbow for Ordinary Time*, 523 pages.
ISBN 978-1-937081-74-4 *Dawn & Dusk Rainbow Prayer*, 775 pages, (includes also the seasons of Advent, Christmas, Lent & Easter)
These two versions of this rendering are arranged in a two-week repeating cycle, with additional readings and traditional songs.

ISBN 978-1-937081-73-7 *Rainbow Prayer*, 175 pages
This abridged version includes an LGBTQ+Catholic calendar
and the Psalms of Saint Francis of Assisi.

These renderings were composed with specifically LGBTQ+ readers in mind. They remain relevant for all people of God.

A warning: If you need the masculine pronouns for God in traditional translations, you will not like this rendering. For the holy name *YHVH* or Yahweh, the Hebrew word for "My Lord" (***Adonai***) is used, pronounced *ah-duh-'nigh*, and the Aramaic word ***Abba*** for Father. See page 4 for the other choices made in this meditation rendering.

printed and distributed by Ingram Books
published by IDJC Press

www.idjc.org

Rainbow Psalms in 30 Days
with Canticles & Sayings of Jesus

Choices Made in this Meditation Rendering	4
Acknowledgements & Sources	5
Stephen Joseph Wolf	7

PSALMS
Suggested for Morning & Evening
1st through the 30th days of the Month

Book 1 – Psalm 1 – 41	8
Book 2 – Psalm 42 – 72	86
Book 3 – Psalm 73 – 89	142
Book 4 – Psalm 90 – 106	182
Book 5 – Psalm 107 – 150	222

CANTICLES 311
Options for Morning & Evening

Sunday	312	315
Monday	316	322
Tuesday	323	330
Wednesday	331	337
Thursday	339	345
Friday	346	354
Saturday	355	363

An Introduction to Prayer	364
More Passages for Prayer from your Bible	365-371
Index of Canticles & Sayings of Jesus	372
Index of Corner Notes, Corner Quoters, & Images	374
Chapter-A-Day Bible Readiing Plan	376
Lectio Divina	377
Petitions	378
The Lord's Prayer	379
Canticle of Zechariah concluding Morning Prayer	380
Canticle of Mary concluding Evening Prayer	381

CHOICES MADE in this MEDITATION RENDERING

The traditional translation of the *Liturgy of the Hours* is a beautiful one for chanting in monasteries. As a former parish priest for twenty-two year, now in retirement, almost all of my time with the Psalter is with the universal People of God but alone with God, whether in my room, in a chapel, or in the woods. Praying in *Lectio Divina,* trying to listen to the Lord, I have found much prayerful fruit in several translations.

The biggest challenge to people new to the *Liturgy of the Hours* is how to do it. The ecumenical *Book of Common Prayer* deals with this quite effectively by simply assigning psalms to consecutive days of the month, from 1 to 30. This book follows that arrangement.

This meditation rendering follows consciously these choices:

1. For the name *YHVH*, or *Yahweh,* the Hebrew word **Adonai** (ah-duh-nigh') meaning *My Lord,* is used. In several places the words *El* or *Elyon* or *Elohim* are retrieved, as is *Sabaoth* instead of *Mighty* or *Hosts.*

2. Following the Christian understanding of one God in the three persons of the Trinity, masculine pronouns for God are avoided (I really don't know why women tolerate them), except when God is referred to as Father, or specific references to Jesus. I do this as an openly gay cis-gender male.

3. Except in the traditional Lord's Prayer and doxology, rather than the Greek **Father** (*pater*) the more intimate Aramaic **Abba** is used (think Dad, Daddy, Papa) as in Mark 14:36. Among my family and friends, no one addresses their Daddy as Father. See also Saint Paul's use of *Abba* in Romans 8:15 and Galatians 4:6.

4. In an admittedly imperfect effort to pray the gospel as well as the psalms, the word *enemy* is most often rendered as *enmity* and *foes* as *adversity.*

5. Where people are referred to as *evil,* the emphasis is shifted to those who *do* the bad, or *ways* that are bad.

6. Since *race* is a human construct, and we are all members of the one human race, words such as *tribe* and *family* are used.

ACKNOWLEDGEMENTS & SOURCES

There are problems with all of these choices. Still, in my judgment, the benefits overwhelm the problems.

Any errors in this rendering are entirely my own. Let us be grateful for all those who do the real work of translating sacred scripture.

Most of the Antiphons are **Sayings of Jesus** drawn from Sunday Gospel readings: In the Sunday Lectionary, the Old Testament readings have connections with the Gospel reading, and the Responsorial Psalm is a response to the Old Testament reading. This means that on any given Sunday there is a relationship between the Gospel reading and the Psalm. The antiphons were chosen based on this relationship.

Some of the **intercessions and petitions** on page 378 are drawn from *Guadium et Spes*, "Pastoral Constitution on the Church in the Modern World," Vatican II, 1965, paragraph 27.

ACKNOWLEDGEMENTS & SOURCES

The primary source for this work is the grace of three decades with the psalms, canticles and readings from many translations, including:

The Liturgy of the Hours (Four Volumes), Copyright © 1974 ICEL International Committee on English in the Liturgy, Inc.

New American Bible with Revised New Testament, (1986) *and* ***Revised Psalms*** (1991) Copyright © 1991, 1986, 1970 Confraternity of Christian Doctrine, Inc. Washington, D.C. All rights reserved. (*This is my favorite translation of the Psalms.*)

New American Bible Revised Edition (NABRE), Copyright © 2010, 1986 Confraternity of Christian Doctrine, Washington, D.C. All rights reserved. (*This is the current Catholic translation.*)

New Revised Standard Version Bible: Catholic Edition, Copyright © 1993 and 1989 by the Division of Christian Education of the National Council of the Churches of Christ in the U.S.A.

The New Jerusalem Bible, Copyright © 1985 by Darton, Longman & Todd, Ltd. & Doubleday, a division of Bantam Doubleday Dell Publishing Group, Inc.

The Jewish Study Bible, Copyright © 1985, 1999 by the Jewish Publication Society

RAINBOW PSALMS IN 30 DAYS

Acknowledgments & Sources, continued

The Interlinear NIV Hebrew-English Old Testament, by John R. Kohlenberger III, Copyright © 1979, 1980, 1982, 1985, 1987 by the Zondervan Corporation

The NRSV-NIV Parallel New Testament in Greek and English, by Alfred Marshall, Copyright © 1990 by the Zondervan Corporation

The New Greek-English Interlinear New Testament, translators Robert K. Brown & Philip W. Comfort, Copyright © 1990 by Tyndale House Publishers

I am especially grateful for these three, and to all those who worked on the *New American Bible* Psalms of 1991.

These works were also very helpful:

The New Jerome Biblical Commentary, edited by Raymond E. Brown, S.S., Joseph A. Fitzmyer, S.J., and Roland E. Murphy, O.Carm., Copyright © 1990, 1968 by Prentice-Hall, Inc.

The following volumes from the **Anchor Bible**:

Psalms I (1-50); Psalms II (51-100); Psalms III (101-150), The Anchor Bible, Volumes 16, 17, and 17A, by Mitchell Dahood, S.J., Copyright © 1965,1966, © 1968, © 1970, Doubleday

The Wisdom of Ben Sira; The Anchor Bible, Vol. 39, by Patrick W. Skehan, Copyright © 1987, Doubleday & Company, Inc.

Tobit; The Anchor Bible, Vol. 40A, by Carey A. Moore, Copyright © 1996, Doubleday

The Wisdom of Solomon; The Anchor Bible, Vol. 43, by David Winston, Copyright © 1979, Doubleday & Company, Inc.

Daniel, Esher and Jeremiah, the Additions; The Anchor Bible, Vol.44, by Carey A. Moore, Copyright © 1977, Doubleday & Company, Inc.

The summary of *Lectio Divina* on page 377 comes from many guides, all of whom have my deep gratitude, expecially Rev. Paul Wachdorf of Mundelein Seminary, north of Chicago.

And a stack of dictionaries.

Stephen Joseph Wolf   Nashville, Tennessee   **www.idjc.org**

Books by Stephen Joseph Wolf

PRAYER BOOKS	FAITH SHARING ETC
Rainbow Prayer	*Pondering Our Faith*
Rainbow Psalms in 30 Days	*Tree of Life*
Dawn & Dusk Rainbow	*Forty Penances for Spiritual Exercise*
* for Ordinary Time*	*The Passion in the Great Story of Jesus*
Dawn & Dusk Rainbow Prayer	*The Resurrection in the...Story of Jesus*
* (ordinary time & the seasons)*	*God's Ones: Living in the Lord*
	Being Spouses
A Jesus Breviary	*God's Money*
31 Days of God's Love-Call	*Twelve-Step Spirituality for Christians*
31 Days of Jesus Sayings	*Anger the Jesus Way*
Pocket Retreat	*Planning My Own Funeral?*

POETRY	*Seeking Holy Honesty*
ESSAY	*Gay Respect in the Good News*
UKULELE SONGBOOKS	*Three-Finger Chord Ukulele Hymns* *Three-Finger Chord Ukulele Old-Timey Songs*

Stephen Joseph Wolf is retired, a former parish priest (22 lents & holy weeks), spiritual director and retreat leader, and former certified public accountant (14 tax seasons), before that working as a landscaper, desk clerk, laundry worker, janitor, paper boy, and student, growing up the second of eight children of a parish secretary and Nashville's best television repairman. He continues to write for faith-sharing groups and retreats, paint folk art icons, sing baritone for the LGBTQ+ chorus *Nashville in Harmony*, play the ukulele with *Music for Seniors* and others, volunteer with *PFLAG Nashville* and as bookkeeper for two non-profits, and lives in Nashville with his husband Billy. **www.idjc.org**

PSALM 1

Antiphon *Blessed are the poor in spirit,*
for theirs is the reign of heaven.   Mt 5:3

Blessings are on the human being
who stands not in selfish counsel,
who walks not the way of sinners,
who sits not in the seat of mockers,
but rather delights in the law of Adonai
and meditates on it by day and by night.

This blessed one is like a tree
planted by streams of water
which yields fruit in the season
and its leaf withers not
and prosperity finds what this one does.

Not so those who do the bad,
but rather like the chaff blown in the wind
those who do the bad
will be unable to stand in the judgment
nor sinners in the assembly of the just.

Adonai watches over the way of the just
and bad ways will perish.

•

A tree gives glory to God by being a tree.
See *New Seeds of Contemplation* by Thomas Merton

Day 1 - MORNING

PSALM 2

Antiphon *Wind blows where it will;*
you hear its sound not knowing
from where it comes and goes away;
so with everyone
who is born of the Spirit.   Jn 3:8

Why do nations rage and peoples plot vanity?
Rulers of the earth make their stand
and rulers gather together
against Adonai and the anointed of Adonai:
"Let us break their chains,
let us throw off their fetters."

The One enthroned in the heavens laughs,
the Lord scoffs and rebukes them.
In anger and in wrath the Lord terrifies them.
"I indeed installed my ruler
on my holy mountain of Zion.

I will proclaim a decree of Adonai who said,
'You are my child, this day I am your abba.
Ask of me and nations are your inheritance,
and your possession to the ends of earth.
You will rule them with a scepter of iron
and dash them to pieces of what potters make.'

Day 1 - MORNING
Psalm 2, continued

Rulers, now be wise!
Royals of earth, be warned!
Serve Adonai with fear; rejoice with trembling!
Kiss my child, lest there be anger
and you be destroyed
for in a moment wrath can flare up.

Blessings on all who take refuge in God."

•

*The contemplative life provides
an area, a space of liberty, of silence,
in which possibilities are allowed to surface
and new choices become manifest.*

See *The Intimate Merton,* by Thomas Merton

Day 1 - MORNING

PSALM 3

Antiphon *Whoever does and teaches
these commandments
will be called great in
the reign of heaven.* Mt 5:19

How many, Adonai,
are rising against me,
saying of me in enmity,
"No deliverance by God for this self!"

But you, Adonai, shield around me,
my glorious One, you lift my head.
My voice cries to Adonai
who answers me from the holy mountain.

I lie down and I sleep;
and I wake because Adonai sustains me.
I will have no fear of tens of thousands of people
who are drawn up on every side against me.

Arise, Adonai! Deliver me, my God!
You struck the jaw of enmity
and broke the teeth of bad doings.
From Adonai is the deliverance.
May your blessing be on your people.

•

PSALM 4

Antiphon *You are witnesses of these things,*
the Christ to suffer,
and rise on the third day.   Lk 24:46

When I call, answer me, saving God.
From distress you give me relief.
Be merciful to me and hear my prayer.

Until when, human, will you shame the glory?
Until when will you love delusion and seek the lie?
Know that Adonai set apart the faithful for Adonai
and will hear when I call.

When you tremble in awe, do not sin.
Search in your heart and on your bed, and be silent.
Offer sacrifices of goodness, and trust Adonai.

Many are asking, "Who can show us good?
Adonai, let the light of your faces shine upon us."

You put joy in my heart, more joy
than when their grain and new wine abound.
In the peace of God's face I will lie down and sleep,
for you alone, Adonai, make me dwell in safety.

•

50 psalms are unattributed. 73 are
attributed to David (about 1,000 BC), 12 each to
sons of Asaph & Korah, 2 of Solomon and one (Ps 90) to Moses.

Day 1 - MORNING

PSALM 5

Antiphon   *If someone wishes to sue you*
to get your tunic,
let that one take also the cloak.   Mt 5:40

Give ear to my words, Adonai;
consider my sighing.
Listen to the sound of my cry for help,
for to you I pray, my Ruler and my God.

Hear, Adonai, my morning voice;
with my morning request before you, I wait.

You are not pleased with doings of the bad,
nor can their doers dwell with you.
The arrogant cannot stand before your eyes.
You hate when wrong is done, you destroy lies,
you abhor bloodshed and deceit.

By the greatness of your mercy, Adonai,
I will come into your house,
In reverence I will bow in your holy temple.

Lead me in your justice, Adonai;
because of enmity
make straight before me your way.

Psalm 5, continued

Their mouth is not to be trusted,
their heart is destruction,
their throat an open grave,
and their tongue speaks deceit.

If you, God, declare them guilty
let their fall be by their intrigue;
let them be banished if they have sinned,
if they have rebelled against you.

But let all who take refuge in you be glad;
let them sing for joy forever.
You spread protection over them
that they may rejoice in you and love your name.

You bless the just, Adonai,
surrounding them with favor as a shield.

• • •

It's letting go
of the sense that the past
should have been any different or better.
See *The Tricky Part* by Martin Moran

Day 1 - EVENING

PSALM 6

Antiphon   *Young human, I say to you: Arise!*   Lk 7:14

Adonai, do not rebuke me in your anger
nor discipline me in your wrath.
Be merciful to me, Adonai, for I am weak.
Heal me, Adonai, for my bones are in agony
and my soul is in great anguish.

But you, Adonai, how long?
Turn, Adonai, and deliver my soul!
Save me because of your unfailing love!
Not from death are you remembered.
Who can praise you from Sheol?

I am worn out from my groaning;
through all the night I flood my bed with tears,
I drench my couch.
My eye grows weak with sorrow;
she weakens because of enmity.

Away from me, all doers of the bad,
for Adonai has heard the sound of my weeping.
Adonai has heard my cry for mercy.
Adonai accepts my prayer.
May enmity be ashamed and greatly dismayed,
and turn back in humble confusion.

•

PSALM 7

Antiphon *Why do you see*
the piece of dust in your neighbor's eye
but ignore the wood beam
in your own eye?   Lk 6:41

My God, **Adonai**, in you I take refuge;
save me and deliver me from all who pursue me.
Like lions they want to tear me up,
rip my self to pieces with no one to save me.

My God, Adonai, if I deserve this,
if there is guilt on my hands,
if I did wrong to one at peace with me,
or if I robbed without cause from an adversary,

then let that one pursue my self
and overtake my life
and trample my honor to the ground;
let that one put me down in the dust.

Arise, Adonai, rise up in your anger
against the rages of enmity.

Awake, my God, and decree your justice
and let the assembly of peoples gather to you;
rule over us from the height.
Let Adonai be the judge of the peoples.

Judge me, Adonai, as you judge me in justice,
as you judge my integrity, Most High.
May violence end now and the just be secure;
search our minds and hearts, God of justice.

My shield, God Most High,
saves the honest of heart,
and judges each day with justice,
holding the threat of wrath.

If none repent, they will sharpen their sword
and bend their bow with string and make ready
with weapons of death and flaming arrows.
See, trouble is conceived and evil is pregnant,
then comes to birth disillusionment.

They dig holes and scoop them out
but fall into the pits they made.
Their trouble recoils on their heads;
on their heads their violence makes landing.

I give thanks for the justice of Adonai
and sing praise to the name of Most High Adonai.

•

---

*The old joke is that though the psalmists seem to suffer from
paranoia, nevertheless somebody might truly be out to get them.*

PSALM 8

Antiphon *I have much more to tell you,
but you cannot bear it yet.* Jn 16:12

Adonai, our Lord!
How majestic is your name in all the earth!

Your glory is set above the heavens!
From lips of children and infants
you ordained strength to bring to silence
enmity, adversity and vengeance.

When I consider your heavens,
the works of your fingers,
the moon and stars which you set in place,
what is a human that you would be mindful,
a child of Adam and Eve that you would care?

And you made us little lower than a "god"
crowning us with glory and honor,
making us to rule over works of your hands,
putting everything under our feet,

all the flocks and herds and beasts of the field,
birds of the air and fishes of the sea,
all that swims through the paths of the seas.

Adonai, our Lord!
How majestic is your name in all the earth!

• • •

Day 2 - MORNING

PSALM 9

Antiphon   *Foxes have holes and birds of the sky nests,*
but the Son of Humanity has no place
where his head may lay.   Lk 9:58

I will praise Adonai with all my heart;
I will tell of all the wonderful things.
I will be glad and rejoice in you,
I will sing praise to your name, Most High.

When enmity turns back
it stumbles before you
for you upheld my right and my cause;
you sat on the throne judging justly.

You rebuked nations, you destroyed bad ways;
their name you blotted out to forever and ever.
Enmity is overtaken by endless ruin;
cities are uprooted and their memories perish.

Adonai reigns to forever,
set up on the throne for judgment
to judge the world in fairness
and to govern peoples with justice.

Adonai is the refuge for the oppressed,
the stronghold in times of trouble.
Those who know your name will trust in you,
for you never forsake seekers of Adonai.

Psalm 9, continued

Sing praise to Adonai, enthroned in Zion.
Proclaim the deeds among the nations
for the One who can avenge violence remembers
and does not ignore the cry of the afflicted.

Have mercy on me, Adonai,
and see the persecution of enmity.
Lift me up from the gates of death
that I may declare all of your praises
in the gates of your daughter Zion.
I will rejoice in your salvation.

Nations fell into the pit they dug;
in the net that they hid are their own feet caught.
Adonai is known by justice;
bad ways get snared in their handiwork.

The nations forgetting God return to Sheol,
but the needy will not be forgotten
nor will the hope of the afflicted ever perish.

Arise Adonai; let not the human triumph.
Let the nations be judged in your presences.
Strike the nations, Adonai,
and let them know their humanity.

•

Live always, monk, as if you were to die tomorrow
but treat the body as if to live on with it for many years to come.
See *Praktikos* (#29) by Evagrius Ponticus

Day 2 - MORNING

PSALM 10

Antiphon — *New wine is put into fresh wineskins.* Mk 2:22

Why, Adonai, do you stand distant
and hide in times of the trouble?
In arrogance doers of the bad hunt the weak
and are caught in schemes they devise.

Doers of the bad boast of what their hearts crave,
blessing the greedy and reviling Adonai.
In pride they point their nose away
and seek God in none of their thoughts.

Their haughty ways prosper always,
your laws are kept at a distance,
and they sneer at all who oppose them.

They say to themselves
"I will not be shaken, but happy,
untroubled for generations to come."
Their mouths are full of curses, lies and threats,
trouble and bad things kept under their tongue.

They lie in wait to ambush villages and murder,
their secret eyes on the innocent victim.
They lie in wait to ambush like a lion,
undercover lying in wait to catch the helpless,
they catch and drag the helpless off in their nets.

Psalm 10, continued

The victims are crushed and collapse,
falling under their strength.
They say to themselves "El has forgotten,
with faces covered, and sees nothing anymore."

Arise, Adonai! God, lift up your hand!
Do not forget the helpless ones.
For why do those doing bad revile God and say,
to themselves, "God will not call an accounting"?

But you do see trouble and grief,
and consider taking the matter in hand;
to you the victims commit themselves,
to you, the helper of orphans.

Stop the arm of the doer of the bad;
call to account lest bad things be kept secret.
Adonai rules forever and ever;
the nations will vanish from the land.

You hear, Adonai, the desire of the afflicted;
you encourage their heart and open your ear
to defend the orphaned and the oppressed.
May humanity repeat no terror on the earth.

•

A subordinate caste accepts a survival mechanism in which people must become attuned to the people with power over them and learn to adjust themselves to their expectations to please them.
See *Caste: the Origins of Our Discontents* by Isabel Wilkerson.

PSALM 11

Antiphon *Blessed are you poor,*
for yours is the reign of God. Lk 6:20b

In Adonai I take refuge.
How can you say to my self,
"Flee, bird, to your mountain
for look, doers of bad now bend their bow,

they set their arrow on the string
to shoot from the shadow at the upright of heart.
When the foundations are destroyed,
what can the upright do?"

Adonai is in the holy temple,
on Adonai's throne in the heavens
with eyes observing, examining
the sons and daughters of humanity.

Adonai examines the good and the bad,
hating in the soul the love of violence,
and will rain onto bad ways
coal and sulphur on fire
and scorching wind, the lot of their cup,

for Adonai is just, loving justice;
we will see the faces of the Just One.

• • •

PSALM 12

Antiphon *A cloud came overshadowing them
and a voice came out of the cloud:
this is my Beloved Son; hear him.*   Mk 9:7

Help, **Adonai**, for the godly are no more;
the faithful vanish from humanity's children.
They speak the lie to each of their neighbors,
lips flattering with a double heart.

May Adonai close all flattering lips
and tongues speaking the boast that say:
"With our tongues we will triumph,
our lips are our own; who is our master?"

But because of oppression of the weak,
because of groaning of the needy,
now Adonai says, "I will arise and protect them."

Words of Adonai are flawless words,
like silver refined in the furnace of clay,
and being purified seven times over.

You, Adonai, you will keep them safe;
you are our protection to forever.
But doers of the bad will still strut about
when vileness is honored among human beings.

•

*In contrast with the Transfiguration, at the Baptism
in Mark and Luke the voice says* You are my Beloved Son.

PSALM 13

Antiphon   *Emmanuel! God is with us!*   Mt 1:23

Until when, Adonai?
Will you forget me to forever?
Until when will you hide your faces from me?
Until when must I wrestle
with thoughts of my soul
and sorrow in my heart by day?
Until when will enmity triumph?

Look! Answer me, my God Adonai!
Give light to my eyes, or I will sleep the death!
Or enmity will say, "I overcame that one,"
and foes will rejoice when I fall.

But my trust is in your unfailing love;
my heart rejoices in your salvation.
I will sing to Adonai, who is good to me.

•

---

*'Until When?' is also
translated 'How Long?'*

PSALM 14

Antiphon *If we say we have no sin,*
we deceive ourselves;
if we confess our sins,
God is faithful and forgiving.   1 John 1:8,9

The fool says in the heart, "There is no God."
They are corrupt, vile are their deeds;
no one is doing good.

Adonai looks down from the heavens
on sons and daughters of Adam and Eve
to see if even one is wise enough to seek God.

All turned aside together to corruption;
no one is doing good, not even one.

Will doers of the bad never learn?
Devouring my people as they eat bread,
they do not call on Adonai.

There they are, in dread of dread,
for God is in the company of the just.
They frustrate the hopes of the poor,
but in Adonai the poor find refuge.

Who from Zion could bring salvation to Israel?
When Adonai restores the fortune to the people,
let Jacob rejoice, let Israel be glad.

• • •

Day 3 - MORNING

PSALM 15

Antiphon *Blessed are the clean of heart,*
for they will see God.   Mt 5:8

Adonai, who may dwell in your tent sanctuary?
Who may live on your holy mountain?
One walking without blame, one doing the right,
speaking the truth in the heart,

whose tongue does not slander,
who does no wrong to a neighbor,
who casts no slur on a mutual human,
in whose eyes vile acts are despised

while those who fear Adonai are honored,
whose sworn oath is not changed even to pain,
who lends money without usury,
and accepts no bribe against the innocent.

One faithful in these
will be unshaken to forever.

•

Humans, you have been told
what is good and what Adonai requires of you:
do justice, love goodness, and walk humbly with your God.
Micah 6:8

PSALM 16

Antiphon *Heaven and earth will pass away,*
but my words will not pass away.   Mk 13:31

Day 3 - MORNING

Keep me safe, *El*, for I take refuge in you.
I said to Adonai, "You are my Lord;
I have no good apart from you."

Worthless are the false gods in the land,
even though some delight in them.
Those who run after other gods
will increase their sorrows;
I will not pour out their blood libations,
nor let their names pass my lips.

Adonai, you assign my portion and my cup;
you make my lot secure.
Boundary lines fall for me in the pleasant places;
surely this inheritance is my delight.

I will praise Adonai who counsels me,
even in the night instructing my heart.
With Adonai before me, always by my side,
I will not be shaken.

And so my heart is glad and my tongue rejoices.
My body will rest in security
because you will not abandon my self to Sheol;
you will not let your faithful one see decay.

You will show me the path of living,
fullness of joy in your presences,
eternal pleasures at your right hand.

•

PSALM 17

Antiphon   *The Lord is God of the living.*   Lk 20:38

Alternate   Now, Master, you set free your servant
according to your word in peace;
my eyes have seen the salvation,
which you have prepared
before the face of all the peoples,
a light for revelation to the nations
and glory for your people, Israel.

Lk 2:29-32
Canticle of Simeon
(*often used in
night prayer*)

Hear, **Adonai**, a just plea; listen to my cry.
Give ear to my prayer, from lips without deceit.
May my vindication come from you;
may my eyes see right things.

You probe and examine my heart in the night,
you test me and find nothing wrong.
By resolve my mouth will not sin.

By the word of your lips
my human deeds are kept from violent ways.
Holding my steps to your paths
my feet did not slip.

Day 3 - MORNING

I call on you, El, for you will answer me.
Give ear to me and hear my prayer.
Show the wonder of your great saving love;
at your right hand are refugees from adversity.

Keep me as the apple daughter of your eye.
You hide me in the shade of your wings
from those who assail me in enmity,
surrounding around my life.
They close their callous hearts,
they speak their arrogant mouth.

Now they surround our tracks;
their eyes are alert, ready to throw to the ground.
They are like a lion, hungry to tear prey,
like a great lion crouching to ambush.

Rise up, Adonai!
Confront and bring down their ways.
Rescue my self by your sword, Adonai,
by your hand from humans,
humans of the world whose reward is this life.

As for those who are cherished by you,
their belly is full, sons and daughters are plenty,
and they store up their wealth for their children.

May justice let me see your faces
and be satisfied waking up to your likeness.

• • •

PSALM 18:2-30

Antiphon *You shall love the Lord, your God*
with all your heart and soul and mind,
and your neighbor as yourself.   Mt 22:37,39
see also
Dt 6:5 & Lev 19:18

I love you, **Adonai**, my strength,
my rock Adonai, my fortress and deliverer;
in my God and Rock I take refuge,
my shield and horn, my salvation and stronghold.

I call out praise to Adonai
and am saved from enmity.

They tangled me in cords of death
and overwhelmed me in torrents of destruction.
Cords of Sheol coiled around me
and snares of death confronted me.

In my distress I called "Adonai,"
I cried for help from my God,
who heard from the temple my voice;
my cry went into these ears.

The earth trembled and quaked
and foundations of mountains shook
and trembled because of anger.
Smoke rose from the nostrils
and fire from the mouth consumed blazing coals.

Day 3 - EVENING

The heavens parted
and dark clouds came down under the feet.
Mounted on the cherub,
flying and soaring on wings of wind,
a canopy of darkness covered all around,
dark waters in the clouds of the skies.

From the brightness of the presence
the clouds advanced hailstone and lightning bolts.
Adonai thundered from the heavens,
the voice of the Most High resounding
as hailstone and lightning bolts.

Arrows shot, scattering them all;
with great lightning bolts they are routed.
Valleys of waters were exposed
and foundations of earth laid bare
at your rebuke, Adonai,
at the blast of the breath of your nostril.

You reached from on high and took hold of me
and drew me out from the deep waters;
you rescued me from enmity
and from those too strong, too powerful for me.

They confronted me in the day of my disaster
but Adonai was my support,
brought me out to the spacious place,
and rescued me because of delight in me.

Psalm 18, continued

Adonai dealt with me as my ways are upright,
rewarded me as my hands are clean,
for I kept to the ways of Adonai.
Indeed all of God's laws are before me
and I did not turn from those decrees.

Blameless before God, on guard against sin,
in the sight of Adonai I am rewarded
as my ways are just and my hands are clean.

To the faithful you show yourself faithful,
to the honest you show yourself honest,
and to the pure you show yourself pure,

but to the crooked you show yourself shrewd,
for you save humble people
but bring low the eyes of the haughty.

Indeed you make my lamp burn;
my God Adonai makes light in my darkness.
Indeed with you I can advance against troops,
with my God I can scale a wall.

•

Our lives become a parchment;
our sufferings and our actions are the ink.
The workings of the Holy Spirit are the pen,
and with it God writes a living gospel.
Jean-Pierre de Caussade, Jesuit

Day 3 - EVENING

PSALM 18:31-51

Antiphon   *Hear, Israel,*
            the Lord our God is One.   Mk 12:29

The ways of God are perfect,
the word of Adonai is flawless,
a shield for all who need refuge.
For who is God besides Adonai?
And who is the Rock except our God?

God arms me with strength,
makes my way good,
makes my feet like the deer
and makes me to stand at full height,
training my hands for the battle;
my arms can bend a bow of bronze.

You give to me your shield of victory,
your right hand sustains me,
stooping to make me great.
You broaden my path beneath me
so my ankles do not turn.

I pursued and overtook enmity
and did not turn back until its defeat…
They fell beneath my feet.

You armed me with strength for the battle
and made the adversity bow at my feet.
You turned back enmity and brought its defeat.

Psalm 18, continued

They cried for help, but no one saved them.
Adonai did not answer them.
I beat them as dust in the wind;
like mud in the streets I poured them out.

You delivered me from attacks of people,
you made me as a head of nations;
people I knew not became subject to me.
Hearing me in their ear they obey.

Foreigners cringe before me, losing heart,
trembling out of strongholds.

Adonai is alive and praised;
may my Rock be exalted, my saving God.
God gives victory to me
and subdues nations under me,

saving me from enmity,
and rescuing me from violence.
I praise you, Adonai, among the nations,
and to your name I will sing praise.

You make great victories of your king
with unfailing kindness to David, your anointed,
and his descendants to forever.

• • •

*If I expect another human to love me perfectly, then
I am expecting them to be God, and I will be disappointed.*

See *Bread for the Journey* by Henri Nouwen

Day 4 - MORNING

PSALM 19

Antiphon *The Samaritan did mercy
to the beaten man;
you go and do likewise.* Lk 10:37

The heavens declare the glory of God,
and the sky proclaims the work of God's hands.
Day after day, speech pouring forth,
knowledge is on display night after night.

There is no speech, there is no language,
and no sound is heard.
Yet into all the earth their line goes out
and their words to the ends of the world.

There God has pitched a tent for the sun,
and like a bridegroom coming forth,
and like an athlete running the course, rejoices.

At the end of the heavens is the rising of the sun,
to their furthest ends is the circuit,
and nothing is hidden from its heat.

The law of Adonai is perfect, reviving the soul;
statutes of Adonai are trustworthy,
making wise of the simple;
precepts of Adonai are right ones,
giving joy of heart;

Psalm 19, continued

the command of Adonai is radiant,
giving light to eyes;
the fear of Adonai is pure, enduring to forever;
ordinances of Adonai are sure and altogether just;

more precious than gold,
much more than pure gold,
sweeter than honey,
the honey of honeycombs.

Your servant is warned by them;
to keep them is a great reward.
Who can discern errors?
From those hidden from me, forgive me!

And keep your servant from willful sins!
May they not control me;
then will I be blameless
and innocent of great transgression.

May the words of my mouth be as pleasing
and the meditation of my heart be as pleasing
before you, Adonai,
my Rock and my Redeemer.

•

And who is my neighbor? (Luke 10:29)
The family living next door to me are neighbors, and
the family next door to them. How far away does someone have
to live to no longer be my neighbor? Jesus says there is no such distance.

PSALM 20

Antiphon
*The Spirit of the Lord is upon me;
the Lord anointed me
to evangelize the poor
and sent me
to proclaim release to captives,
sight to the blind,
and freedom to the crushed,
to proclaim a year
of the Lord's acceptance.*

Lk 4:18
and see Isaiah
61:1-2 & 58:6

---

*What
is justice? The
root of justice is in the
awareness that God created an
abundance intended as a blessing for all.
If anyone is denied their just due of this abundance
our God has given for us all, that is injustice. The ancient
Hebrew test for whether we live in a just society is to ask how
the widows, orphans, and alien strangers in our midst are doing.*

Deal with your neighbor with justice; oppress no alien, orphan, or widow; shed no innocent blood; and follow no other "god."
Jeremiah 7:5b,6

Day 4 - MORNING

Psalm 20

May Adonai answer you on the day of distress.
May the name of the God of Jacob protect you,
send you help from the sanctuary,

support you from Zion,
remember all of your sacrifices,
accept your burnt offerings,
give to you as your heart desires,
and make all of your plans succeed.

We will shout for joy at your victory
and lift a banner in the name of our God;
may Adonai grant all your requests.

Now I know
that Adonai saves the chosen anointed
and answers from the holy heavens
with a strong hand of saving powers.

Some trust in the chariot
and others in the horses,
but we in the name of our God Adonai.
They kneel and they fall,
but we rise up and stand firm.

Adonai, save the ruler;
answer us on the day we call.

•

In the name of the Abba and
of the Son and of the Holy Breath of God

Day 4 - MORNING

PSALM 21:2-8,14

Antiphon *Jesus and his disciples ate at the house of Levi and with them tax collectors and sinners; many from there followed him.* Mk 2:15

In your strength, Adonai, the crown rejoices,
and in your victory; how great is the joy!
You granted the desire of their heart
and did not withhold the request of their lips.

Indeed, you welcomed them with rich blessings
and placed on their head a crown of pure gold.
They asked from you life
and you gave length of days forever and ever.

Great is the glory through your victory;
on them you bestowed splendor and majesty.
Surely you granted them blessings for eternity
making them glad with joy in your presences,

for the ruler trusting in Adonai will be unshaken
through the unfailing love of the Most High…
Be exalted, Adonai, in your strength!
We will sing and we will praise your might.

• • •

Being homosexual is not a crime.
Pope Francis, January 24, 2023

PSALM 22

Antiphon *I am the true vine*
and my Abba is the vinegrower.   Jn 15:1

My God, **my God**, why have you forsaken me?
Far from my salvation are the words of my groan.
My God, I cry out by day, but you do not answer,
and at night with no relief.

Yet you Holy One are enthroned, praises Israel.
In you our ancestors trusted and were delivered.
To you they cried and they were saved.
In you they trusted and were not disappointed.

But I am a worm and a no-human,
the scorn of humanity and despised by people.
All those seeing me mock at me;
they shake their heads in insult:
"In the one you trust, let your Adonai rescue you;
let the one who 'delights' in you deliver you!"

You brought me out from the womb,
to trust in you at the breasts of my mother.
From the womb I was cast upon you;
from the womb of my mother, you are my God.
Be not far from me,
for trouble is near with no one to help.

Many bulls surround me;
the strong of Bashan encircle me.
They open wide their mouths against me,
lions tearing up prey and roaring.

Like the waters I am poured out
and my bones are all out of joint.
My heart like wax melts away within my insides.

Like a broken clay pot, my strength is dried up,
and my tongue is stuck in the roof of my mouth;
you lay me in the dust of death.
Dogs indeed surround around me,
a band of doers of the bad encircles me as a lion
ready to tear into my hands and my feet.

I can count all of my bones;
they stare and they gloat over me.
They divide my garments among them
and for my clothing they cast lots.

But you, Adonai, be not far off;
come quickly to help me, my Strength!
Deliver my precious life from the sword
and from the power of the dog.
Rescue me from the mouth of the lion
and from the horns of wild oxen.

I will declare your name to my siblings
and praise you within the assembly.

Psalm 22, continued

You fearing Adonai, give praise!
All you descendants of Jacob, give honor!
All you descendants of Israel, give reverence
before Adonai, who despised not, nor disdained,
nor hid the holy face from those suffering affliction,
but heard their cry for help.

From you comes my praise in the great assembly;
my vows will I fulfill before those who fear you.
The poor ones will eat to satisfaction,
and the seekers will praise Adonai;
may your heart live to forever.

All the ends of the earth
will remember and turn to Adonai,
and all the families of nations will bow down,
for to Adonai is the dominion, ruling over nations.
All those rich on the earth will feast and worship
and kneel, all will go down to the dust,
all who cannot keep their own self alive.

Those to come will be served by being told,
and in the same way serve generations to come.
They will come and they will proclaim
the deeds of the fidelity of the Lord,
the story, to people yet to be born.

•

PSALM 23

Antiphon *For I was hungry and you gave me to eat,*
thirsty and you gave me drink,
a stranger and you welcomed me,
naked and you clothed me,
ill and you cared for me,
in prison and you visited me.   Mt 25:35,36

Adonai is my shepherd; nothing do I lack.
My Lord lays me down in green pastures
and leads me beside still quiet waters,
restoring my soul and guiding me
in paths of justice for the Lord's own namesake.

So when I walk in the deep dark valley
I will not fear for you are with me,
your rod and staff a comfort to me.

A table you prepare before me
in the presence even of enmity.
My head you anoint with oil
and my cup is overflowing.

Surely goodness and love will follow me
all the days of my life
and I will dwell in the Lord's own house
for length of days.

• • •

PSALM 24

Antiphon *She will bear a son,*
and you will name him Jesus;
he will save his people from their sins. Mt 1:21

Day 5 - MORNING

The earth and everything,
the world and all who are alive are Adonai's,
God who founded the earth on the seas
and established the earth on the waters.

Who may ascend to the mountain of Adonai?
And who may stand in the holy place?
The clean of hand and pure of heart
who do not lift the soul to an idol
and do not swear by falsehood
will receive the blessing from Adonai
and vindication from the God who saves.

Such is the generation of ones who seek,
who seek your faces, God of Jacob.

Lift up your heads, you gates;
lift up, you ancient doors,
that the Crown of glory may enter.

Who is this Crown of glory?
Adonai, strong and mighty,
Adonai, mighty of battle.

Lift up your heads, you gates;
lift up, you ancient doors,
that the Crown of glory may enter.

Who is this Crown of glory?
Adonai Sabaoth is the Crown of glory.

•

PSALM 25

Antiphon   *The time is full*
and the reign of God has drawn near;
repent and believe in the gospel.   Mk 1:15

To you, **Adonai**, I lift up my soul;
in you, my God, I trust; let me not be shamed
and let enmity not triumph over me.
Indeed all who hope in you will not be shamed;
shamed will be those doing wanton treachery.

Show me your ways, Adonai; teach me your paths.
Guide me in your truth and teach me,
for you are my saving God;
you are my hope all the day.

Remember your mercies, Adonai,
and your loves, for they are from of old.
The sins of my youth and rebellious ways
you do not remember, as you are loving.

You do remember me, for you are good, Adonai.
Good and upright is Adonai,
who instructs sinners in the way,
guides humble ones in the right,
and teaches the way to the humble.

Day 5 - MORNING

All the ways of Adonai are loving and faithful
for those who keep the covenant demands.
For the sake of your name, Adonai,
now you forgive my iniquity, great as it is.

Who is the human who fears Adonai?
The one being instructed in the Lord's chosen way,
whose life will be days spent in prosperity,
whose descendants will inherit the land,
the confidence of Adonai is with those thus fearing;
the covenant is made known to them.

My eyes are ever on Adonai,
who will free my feet from the snare.
Turn to me! Be gracious to me!
For I am lonely and afflicted.

Troubles of my heart have multiplied;
free me from my anguish!
Look upon my affliction and distress!
Take away all of my sins!

See the enmity, the increase of fierce hate!
Guard my life! Rescue me!
Let me not be shamed, for I take refuge in you.
May integrity and honesty protect me
because I hope in you.

Redeem Israel, God, from all our troubles.

•

PSALM 26

Antiphon *The tax collectors and prostitutes
are going into the reign of God
before you.* Mt 21:31

Vindicate me, Adonai,
for I have walked blameless in my life
and in Adonai I trusted without waver.

Test me, Adonai! And try me!
Examine my heart and my mind!
For your love is before my eyes
and I walk in your truth.

I do not sit with humans of deceit
nor consort with hypocrites.
I abhor the assembly of those who do the bad,
and do not sit with them.

I wash my hands in innocence
and go about your altar, Adonai,
to proclaim a voice of praise
and to tell of all your wonderful deeds.

Adonai, I love the living place of your house,
the dwelling place of your glory.

Day 5 - MORNING

Take not my soul away with sinners
nor my life with people doing bloody things,
those who scheme in their hands
with their right hand full of bribes.

But I walk blameless in my life.
Redeem me! Be merciful to me!
My foot stands on level ground;
in great assemblies I will praise Adonai.

• • •

As the psalms
serve well for private
prayer, they are even more
a prayer for the people of God
and for the whole world. But when a
psalm seems to not apply to my life today,
I can simply step in another's shoes and pray in
the stead of someone who is feeling so strongly these
very emotions that they cannot bring themselves to pray.

PSALM 27

Antiphon
*Come after me,
and I will make you
fishers of human beings.*   Mt 4:19

Adonai is my light and my salvation.
Whom shall I fear?
Adonai is the stronghold of my life.
Of whom shall I be afraid?

When people doing the bad
advance against me to devour my flesh,
when enmity and adversity go against me,
they will stumble and fall.

Though an army encamp against me,
my heart will not fear.
Though war break out against me,
in this I will be confident.

One thing I ask of Adonai:
to seek and to dwell in Adonai's house,
to gaze on Adonai's beauty
all the days of my life as a seeker in the temple.

I will be kept safely dwelling,
hidden in the shelter of the tabernacle,
on the day of trouble set high upon rock.

Then will my head be lifted above enmity,
and I will sacrifice at the tabernacle
the sacrifice of shouts of joy.

I will sing and make music to Adonai.
Hear, Adonai, my voice calling;
be merciful; answer me.
To you my heart says, "My face seeks you."

Your faces, Adonai, I will seek.
Hide not your faces from me;
turn not away from your servant in anger.

You are my help;
neither reject nor forsake me,
God of my salvation.
Even if my father and my mother forsake me,
you, Adonai, will take me in.

Teach me your way, Adonai,
and lead me through oppression to level paths.
Do not give me over to the desires
of enmity rising with false witnesses
and breathers of violence.

Still I am confident: I will see
the goodness of Adonai in the land of the living.
Wait for Adonai!
Take courage and strengthen your heart.
And wait for Adonai!

•

Day 5 - EVENING

Day 5 - EVENING

PSALM 28:1-3,6-9

Antiphon *Pray for all, even for those in authority,*
that our living may include
quiet and dignity. 1 Tim 2:2

To you I call, my Rock Adonai,
turn not to me a deaf ear.
For if you remain silent, away from me,
then I will be like one going into the pit.

Hear the sound of my cries for mercy
calling to you for help as I lift my hands
toward the Holy Place of your Holiness.

Drag me not away with those who do the bad,
who speak cordiality with their neighbors
but with malice in their heart.

Praised be Adonai,
who heard the sound of my cries for mercy.
Adonai, my strength and my shield,
in whom my heart trusts,
I am helped and my heart leaps for joy
and in my song I will give thanks.

Adonai is the strength
and the saving refuge of the anointed.
Save your people! Bless your inheritance!
Be their shepherd and carry them to forever!

•

PSALM 29

Antiphon *A voice out of heaven:*
this is my Beloved Son
in whom I am well pleased.   Mt 3:17

Day 5 - EVENING

Ascribe to Adonai, you in the heavens,
acknowledge Adonai as glory and strength.
Give to Adonai the glory of the Name.
Worship Adonai in holy splendor.

The voice of Adonai over the waters,
the God of glory thunders.
Adonai over mighty waters,
the voice of Adonai in power and majesty,
the voice of Adonai breaking cedars,

Adonai breaks the cedars of Lebanon
and makes Lebanon leap like a calf
and Sirion like a young bull.

The voice of Adonai strikes flashes of lightning,
the voice of Adonai shakes the desert,
Adonai shakes the desert of Kadesh.

The voice of Adonai makes the deer give birth
and strips the forests bare,
and all in the temple cry, "glory."
Adonai sits over the flood
and Adonai is enthroned as Ruler to forever.

May Adonai give strength to the people;
may Adonai bless the people with peace.

• • •

God is not nice. God is not an uncle. God is an earthquake.
Hasidic saying

PSALM 30

Antiphon *Who touched my garments?* Mk 5:30

I will exalt you, **Adonai**, for you lifted me
and did not let enmity gloat over me.

Adonai, my God, I cried to you for help
and you healed me.
Adonai, you brought my self up from Sheol;
you spared me from going into the pit.

Sing to Adonai, you saints!
Sing praise to the holy name!
One moment in anger,
lifetimes in the Lord's favor;
when through the night weeping abides,*
joy can rejoice in the morning.

I said in complacent security,
I will be unshaken to forever.
In your favor, Adonai,
you made me stand firm as a mountain;
you hid your faces and I was dismayed.

To you, Adonai, I called
and to you, Lord, I cried for mercy.
What would be the gain in my destruction?
What is gained if I go into the pit?

Will the dust praise you?
Will the dust proclaim your fidelity?
Hear, Adonai! Be merciful to me!
Be my one helper, Adonai!

You turned my wailing into dancing;
you removed my sackcloth and clothed me in joy
so that my heart may sing to you,
and not be silent.
My God Adonai, I will thank you to forever.

•

*Some of the Fathers
and Mothers of the Desert
recited all 150 psalms daily.
Saint Benedict (d. 547 AD)
in his monastic Rule laid out a
pattern of praying all the psalms
over each week. Different religious
orders used different versions, including
Saint Francis of Assisi who developed a shorter
breviary of psalm fragments designed to be easy to
carry and Saint Ignatius of Loyola who wanted the
Jesuits to be more free when working with the poor.
The Roman Breviary promulgated in 1568 had many
revisions. The Second Vatican Council led to a four-week
cycle, which is again being updated as this work is concluded.*
See *A Simple Family Breviary From the Psalms of Saint Francis*
by Stephen Joseph Wolf and *The Rule of Saint Benedict*

**When weeping
spends the night
joy may come
in the morning.*
See *Being There*
by Peter Keese

PSALM 31:1-17,20-25

Antiphon   *Everyone who hears my words and does them*
           will be like a wise human
           who built the house on rock.   Mt 7:24

In you, **Adonai**, I take refuge;
let me never be shamed.
Deliver me in your justice.
Quickly turn to me your ear! Rescue me!

Be for me a rock of refuge,
a fortress house to save me.
Since you are my rock and my fortress,
for the sake of your name
you lead me and guide me.

You free me from the trap they set for me,
for you are my refuge.
Into your hands I commend my spirit;
you redeem me, Adonai God of truth.

I hate when humans cling to worthless idols,
and I trust in Adonai.
I will rejoice in your love and be glad
for you saw my affliction;
you knew the anguishes of my soul.

Day 6 - MORNING

You do not put me into hands of enmity;
you set my feet in the spacious place.

Be merciful to me, Adonai, in my distress;
my eyes and my soul and my body
grow weak with sorrow.

My life is consumed by anguish
and my years with groaning.
My strength fails because of my guilt
and my bones grow weak.

Because of enmity I am
the utter contempt of even my neighbors
and a dread to my friends
who see me on the street and flee.

I am forgotten as though dead;
my heart became like broken pottery,
for I hear the slander of many
and terror on every side
when they conspire together against me
and plot to take my life.

But I trust in you, Adonai;
I say you are my God;
my times are in your hand.
Deliver me from the hands
of enmity and pursuers.

Shine your faces on your servant!
Save me in your unfailing love!...

Psalm 31, continued

How great is the goodness
you store up for ones who fear you
and bestow on those taking refuge in you
in the sight of the children of humanity.

You hide them in the shelter of your presence;
from human intrigues you keep them
in a dwelling safe from the strife of tongues.

Adonai is praised for showing wonderful love
to me in the city besieged, and I said in my alarm,
"I am cut off from before your eyes."
Yet you heard the sound of my cries for mercy
when I called to you for help.

Love Adonai, all you saints,
Adonai faithful and preserving,
but paying back in full the arrogant.

Be strong and strengthen your heart,
all you hoping in Adonai!

• • •

*God calls…where your deep
gladness meets the world's deep hunger.*

Frederick Buechner

Day 6 - MORNING

Principle & Foundation:

Life is mostly about learning
to live with God so to love as God loves.
Things are God-gifts for knowing and loving God;
things clung to my center lose this God-given purpose.
In a balanced life every blessing and woe
can help me say a deeper 'Yes' to God.
May my one desire remain to choose each choice
that leads to me becoming God's mercy alive.

See *The Spiritual Exercises* (#23) of St. Ignatius of Loyola, d. 1556

PSALM 32

Antiphon *Do you see this woman?*
Her many sins have been forgiven,
and so she has loved much. Lk 7:44,47

Blessed is the one forgiven of faults,
no longer covered with sin.
Blessed is the human
against whom Adonai does not count sin,
and in whose spirit there is no deceit.

When I kept silent, my bones wasted away
through my groaning all day.
For by day and night
your hand was heavy upon me;
my strength withered as in dry summer heat.

I acknowledged my sin to you,
and did not cover up my iniquity;
I said I will confess my faults to Adonai
and you forgave the guilt of my sin.

For this let every godly one pray to you
at the time to find you.
Surely the rising of mighty waters
will not reach this one.
You are the hiding place for me;
you will protect me from trouble
and surround me with deliverance song.

Day 6 - EVENING

I will instruct you and I will teach you
and counsel you in the way you should go,
keeping an eye on you.

Do not be like a horse
or like your mule with no understanding;
by bit and bridle and harness they are controlled
or else they will not even come to you.

Many woes have doers of the bad,
but the truster in Adonai
is surrounded in unfailing love.

Rejoice in Adonai!
Just ones, be glad!
And sing, all you upright of heart!

•

Principles Toward
Harmony of Tensions:
1. Time is greater than space.
2. Unity prevails over conflict.
3. Realities are greater than ideas.
4. The whole is greater than the part.

See *The Joy of the Gospel* by Pope Francis

PSALM 33

Antiphon *Where your treasure is,*
there also will your heart be. Lk 12:34

Sing joyfully to Adonai, you just,
for praise is fitting for the upright.

Praise Adonai with a harp,
make music on the lyre of ten.
Sing a new song with skill
and play with a shout of joy.

For true is the word of Adonai
and all the faithful deeds done.
The earth is full of the goodness of Adonai,
who loves justice and integrity.

The heavens were made by the word of Adonai
and all their hosts by the breath of the mouth,
as one gathers in a heap the waters of the sea,
as one puts into the deep of the storehouses.

Let all the earth, let them fear,
let all alive in the world revere Adonai
who spoke and it came to be,
who commanded and it stood firm.

Adonai foils the plans of the nations
and thwarts the designs of peoples.
The plan of Adonai stands firm to forever,
heartfelt thoughts to generation and generation.

Day 6 - EVENING

Blessed is the nation for whom Adonai is God,
the people chosen for this inheritance.
From the heavens Adonai looks down and sees
all sons and daughters of Adam and Eve,

and from the place of dwelling watches
all those alive on the earth.
The one who formed our heart
knows all our deeds.

No ruler is saved by the size of an army;
no warrior escapes by greatness of strength.
The horse is a vain hope for deliverance;
despite greatness of strength it cannot save.

See the eye of Adonai on those who place
their fear and hope in the unfailing love
that delivers them from death
and keeps them alive in famine.

Our being waits for Adonai,
who is our help and our shield,
in whom our heart rejoices,
the holy name in whom we trust.

Adonai, may you rest on us your unfailing love
even as we hope in you.

•

When God looks at us God sees Jesus,
and only Jesus, the innocent, guiltless Jesus.
See *Who Told You That You Were Naked?* by John Jacob Raub

PSALM 34

Antiphon *The bread that I will give
is my flesh for the life of the cosmos.* Jn 6:51b

I will extol Adonai at all times,
praise always on my lips.
My soul she will boast in Adonai,
let afflicted ones hear and let them rejoice.

Glorify Adonai with me!
Let us exalt the name together.
I sought Adonai, who answered me
and delivered me from all my fears.

They look to the Name and are radiant;
their faces are never covered with shame.
Adonai heard this poor human call
and saved me from all the troubles.

An angel encamps around
and delivers all who fear Adonai.
Taste and see that Adonai is good!
Blessed is the one who takes this refuge.

Fear Adonai, you saints;
for those who do so there is no lack.
Lions may grow weak and may grow hungry,
but seekers of Adonai lack no good thing.

Day 6 - EVENING

Come, children! Listen to me!
I will teach you the fear of Adonai.
Who is the human who loves living?
Who desires days to see the good?

Keep your tongue from evil
and your lips from speaking the lie.
Turn from the bad and do the good.
Seek and pursue peace.

The eyes of Adonai are on the just
with ears open to their cry.
The faces of Adonai turn from doers of the bad
to cut off from the earth their memory.

They cry and Adonai hears
and delivers them from all their troubles.
Close is Adonai to the brokenhearted,
saving those whose spirit is crushed.

Many are the troubles of the just
but Adonai delivers them from all of them,
protecting all of their bones;
not one of them will be broken.

The bad will slay the bad
and condemned will be those who hate the just.
The servants of Adonai are being redeemed
and the lives of any who take refuge in God
will not be condemned.

• • •

PSALM 35:1-2c,3c,9-19,22-23,27-28

Antiphon   *The tax collector standing far off*
would not lift his eyes to heaven,
but beat his breast saying,
'God, be merciful to me, a sinner.'   Lk 18:13

Contend, **Adonai**, with my contenders!
Restrain those who would attack!
Take up shield and buckler and arise to my aid!...
Say to my soul, "I am your salvation."...

Then my soul will rejoice in Adonai
and take delight in salvation.
All of my bones will exclaim, "Adonai!
Who, like you, rescues the poor from the strong?
or the poor and the needy from robbers?"

Ruthless witnesses come forward;
on things I do not know they question me.
They repay me bad for the good; forlorn is my soul.

Yet when they were ill I clothed myself in sackcloth
and humbled myself with fasting when
my prayer had returned to my breast unanswered.
As a friend and a sibling I went about weeping,
bowing down like a grieving mother.

Luke 18:13 is the source of the popular Jesus Prayer:

But at my stumbling they took glee
and gathered and gathered attackers
and did not cease to slander me unaware,
an ungodly circle of mockers
gnashing their teeth against me.

Until when, Lord? How long will you look on?
Rescue my life from the ravages,
my precious life from the lions.
I will give you thanks in the great assembly;
among people thronging I will praise you.

Let enmity neither gloat without cause or reason
nor wink the eye at me…

You have seen, Adonai; be not silent.
Be not far from me, Lord.
Awake!, my God and Lord,
and rise to my defense.
Vindicate me, Adonai, in your justice…

May those who delight in my vindication
shout and be glad and always say,
"May Adonai be exalted,
who delights in the well being of a servant."
My tongue will tell of your justice
and speak praise of you all the day.

•

Lord Jesus Christ, Son of the Living God, have mercy on me, a sinner

PSALM 36

Antiphon *Blessed are your eyes for they see
and your ears for they hear
what many prophets and just ones
longed to see and hear.* Mt 13:16,17a

An oracle of sin in the midst of my heart:
There is no fear of God in the eyes of a sinner,
whose own eyes are full of self-flattery,
who hates to detect sin.

Words of this mouth are bad and deceitful:
Ceasing to be wise or do good,
they plot the bad while still in bed
and commit to a course of the no-good
and reject nothing that is wrong.

Adonai, to the heavens is your love
and your fidelity to the skies.
Your justice is like the mountains,
your judgment, deep and great;
human and beast you preserve, Adonai.

How priceless is your unfailing love.
High ones and humans find refuge
in the shadow of your wings.

Day 7 - MORNING

They feast on the abundance of your house;
in the river of your delights you give them drink.
With you is the fountain of life,
and in your light we see light.

Continue your love to those who know you
and your just defense of the honest of heart.
Let the foot of pride not come to me
nor the hand of bad ways drive me away.

See, doers of the bad lie fallen;
they are thrown down, unable to rise.

• • •

—
True
Humility
is the grace of
awareness of how I am
created uniquely in God's
image, seeing myself as neither
better than I am nor less than I am.
Humility is reality; pride is an illusion.
Debasement of the self is also an illusion.

PSALM 37

Antiphon *There is nothing entering from outside
that can defile a human;
rather things that defile
come from within.*   Mk 7:15

Fret not over those who do the bad;
envy not those who do wrong.
For like grass their efforts will soon wither,
and like the green plant they wilt away.

Trust in Adonai and do good!
Dwell in the land and enjoy safe pasture!
Delight in Adonai
who will give the desires of your heart.

Commit your way and your trust
to Adonai who will do it:
making your integrity shine like the dawn
and your justice like the noonday sun.

Be still before Adonai and wait with patience.
Fret not over the ways of the successful,
over schemes carried out by human beings.

Refrain from anger and turn from wrath!
Fret not; it brings only the bad,
for humans doing the bad will be cut off;
those who hope in Adonai will inherit the land.

Day 7 - EVENING

A little while and bad doings will be no more;
you will look and not find them in their places.
But the meek will inherit the land
and they will enjoy greatness of peace.

Plotters of bad things to do to the just
gnash their teeth at them.
But the Lord laughs at them,
knowing their day is coming.

They draw their sword and bend their bow
to bring down the poor and the needy,
to slay those of the honest way.
Their sword will pierce into their own heart
and their bows will be broken.

Better the little bit of the just
than the wealth of many who do the bad,
for the powers of bad doers will be broken
while Adonai upholds the just.

Adonai knows the days of the blameless
and their inheritance will endure to forever.
They will not wither in times of disaster
and in days of famine they will enjoy plenty.

But bad ways will perish
and those who choose enmity with Adonai
will vanish like the beauty of fields;
like smoke they will vanish.

Psalm 37, continued

A doer of the bad borrows and does not repay,
but the just are generous and giving.
Their blessing is to live in the land;
but the curse of doing the bad is to be cut off.

The steps of human beings are made firm
by Adonai who delights in their way.
Though we stumble, we will not fall
for Adonai upholds us by the hand.

I was young and now I am old,
yet never have I seen the just forsaken
or their children begging bread.
Generous and lending all the day,
their children are a blessing.

Turn from the bad and do the good!
Then live to always!
For Adonai loves justice
and will not forsake the faithful…
The just will inherit the land
and they will dwell in her to forever.

The mouth of the just he utters wisdom
and the tongue she speaks justice.
The law of their God is in their heart
and their feet do not slip.

Bad ways lie in wait for the just,
seeking to kill them;
Adonai will not leave them under this power
nor let them be condemned when on trial.

Wait for Adonai and keep to the way
of the one who will exalt you to possess the land,
and you will see bad ways cut off.

I saw a ruthless human flourishing
like a native green tree,
but passing away is seen no more;
though I looked he was not to be found.

Consider the honest and observe the upright
for the future is for the person of peace.
But sinners sinning will be destroyed together;
the future of bad ways will be cut off.

The salvation of the just is from Adonai,
their stronghold in times of trouble.
Their help and deliverance and salvation,
their deliverance from ways that are bad,
is Adonai in whom they take refuge.

• • •

'Out from within the human heart come bad thoughts, unchastities, thefts, murders, adulteries, greeds, bad deeds, deceits, lewdness, envies, blasphemy, arrogance and folly.' (Mk 7:21,22) So this saying could also be called the parable of the latrine, as our collective selfishness craps all over creation.

PSALM 38

Antiphon *If a house be divided against itself,
that house will be unabe to stand.* Mk 3:25

Adonai, rebuke me not in your anger
nor discipline me in your wrath,
for your arrows have pierced into me
and your hand has come down upon me.

There is no health in my body
because of your anger;
my bones ache because of my sin.
Indeed my guilts overwhelm my head
like a heavy burden, too heavy for me.

I loathe them and they fester my wounds
because of my foolishness.
I am bowed down and brought very low;
all the day I go about mourning.

Indeed my backside is filled with searing
and there is no health in my body.
Numb and utterly crushed,
my heart groans in anguish.

Lord, before you is all of my longing;
my sighing is not hidden from you.
My heart pounds, my strength fails me,
and my eyes are without their light.

My friends and companions from the past
avoid being present to my woundedness,
and my neighbors stay far away.
People seeking my life set traps;
wanting to harm me, they talk of ruins
and plot deceptions all the day.

I am like the deaf and cannot hear,
like a mute unable to open my mouth.
I became like one who does not hear,
like one whose mouth gives no reply.

Indeed, I wait for you, Adonai;
you will answer, Lord my God.
For I said, "let them not gloat over me
nor puff themselves up when my foot does slip."

For my fall is near; my pain is ever with me.
Indeed I confess my iniquity
and am troubled by my sin.

Vigorous ones seek enmity;
many and numerous hate me for no reason.
When I seek the good they slander me,
repaying the good with the bad.

Forsake me not, Adonai;
my God, be not far from me.
Come quickly to help, my Lord, my salvation.

•

PSALM 39

Antiphon *You are the salt of the earth;*
you are the light of the cosmos.   Mt 5:13a,14a

I said, "I will watch my ways
of sinning with my tongue;
I will put on my mouth a muzzle
as long as temptation is in my presence."
So in silent stillness I said nothing,
and still my anguish increased.

My heart grew hot inside me;
in my meditation a fire burned.
I spoke with my tongue,
"Show me, Adonai, my end,
what is the number of my days;
let me know how fleeting I am.

See the handbreadths you made!
My days and my span are as nothing before you.
Indeed, each of all humanity stands as a breath.
Indeed, as a phantom the human goes out.
Indeed, vainly bustling about, heaping up wealth
without knowing who will get it."

Day 8 - MORNING   81

But what am I looking for now, Lord?
My hope she is in you.
Save me from all my transgressions!
Make me not the scorn of fools.
I was silent and opened not my mouth,
for you, you have done it.

Remove your scourge from me;
from the touch of your hand I am overcome.
With a rebuke for sin you discipline the human
and you consume our wealth like a moth;
indeed we are each but a breath.

Hear my prayer, Adonai, and my cry for help;
listen, El, and be not deaf to my weeping.
For I am with you as a passing guest,
an alien stranger like all my ancestors.
Look away from me that I may rejoice
before I depart and am no more.

●

Look around to ask:
*In years to come when I
look back on my life in these
days, what will I wish had gotten
just a little bit more of my attention?*

PSALM 40:2-14,17-18

Antiphon   *I have come to throw fire on the earth*
and how I wish it was ablaze.   Lk 12:49

Waiting, I waited for Adonai,
who turned to me and heard my cry,

who lifted me from the slime pit
and from the muddy mire,
and set my feet on rock,
making firm my standing place,

and put in my mouth a new song,
a hymn of praise to our God.
Many will see and fear and trust Adonai.

Blessed is the one who trusts in Adonai
and looks not to the proud
or those turning to false "gods."

Adonai, my God, many are your deeds of wonder
and your plans cannot be equaled.
Should I speak and tell of them
they would be too many to declare.

Sacrifice and offerings you did not desire,
but my ears you keep open for me.
Burnt offering and sin offering you did not require.
Then I said, "Here, I have come;

Day 8 - MORNING

in the scroll, in the book, it is written of me.
To do your will, my God, is my desire,
and your law is within my heart."

Your deed I proclaim in the great assembly.
See my lips unsealed; you, Adonai, you know!

I do not hide in my heart what you do;
your faithfulness and your salvation I speak.
I do not conceal your love and your truth
from the great assembly.

Adonai, withhold not your mercies from me,
may your love and your truth protect me always
for countless troubles surround around me.

My sins overtake me and I cannot see.
They are more than the hairs of my head
and my heart fails me.

Be pleased, Adonai, to save me;
Adonai, come quickly to help me!...

May all who seek you rejoice in you and be glad
and may lovers of your salvation say always,
"Let God be exalted."

Yet I am poor and needy.
May the Lord think of me and not delay,
my help and my deliverer, my God.

• • •

PSALM 41

Antiphon *Is it easier to say to the paralytic,*
your sins are forgiven,
or to say, rise and walk?
That you may know
that the Son of Humanity
has authority to forgive sins on earth,
to you paralyzed I say,
'rise; take your mat
and go to your house.' Mk 2:9-11

Blessed are they
who give regard to the weak.
In the time of trouble Adonai will deliver.
Adonai will protect their life,
preserve it blessed in the land,
and give no surrender to the desire of enmity.
Adonai will sustain on the sickbed,
and restore on the bed from all illness.

Adonai, have mercy on me!
Heal my self for I have sinned against you!
Enmity asks in malice:
"When will that one die and be forgotten?"
When they come to see me,
they speak with false hearts, gather slander,
and then go out to the outside to speak.

Together against me they whisper,
imagining the worst for me:
"A vile disease has set in;
that one will not recover."
Even my close friend
has lifted the heel against me,
the human being I trusted,
who ate of my own bread.

But you, Adonai, have mercy on me
and raise me up that I may repay them.
In this I know that you are pleased with me,
for enmity does not triumph over me;
in my integrity you hold me up
and set me in your presences to forever.

Blessed be Adonai, God of Israel,
from everlasting to the everlasting.
Amen and amen.

●

If sometimes people
have had to die of starvation, it is not
because God didn't care for them, but because
you and I were not instruments of love in the hands
of God, to give them bread, because we did not recognize
when once more the hungry Christ came in distressing disguise.
Saint Teresa of Kolkata, d. 1997

PSALM 42

Antiphon *When the shepherd sends them forth
and goes before them, the sheep follow
because they know this voice.*   Jn 10:4

As a deer breathes heavy for streams of water,
so my soul throbs for you, God.

My soul she thirsts for God, the living God.
When can I go and meet the faces of God?

My tears were food for me by day and by night,
while all day they said to me,
"Where is your God?"

These things I remember
as my soul pours out before me:
How I would go with the multitude
to lead them to the house of God
sounding shouts of joy and thanksgiving,
a festive throng!

Why are you downcast, my soul?
Why are you disturbed within me?
Put hope in God, whom I will yet praise,
the saving help and presence.

My God, within me my soul she is downcast.
For this I will remember you
from the land of Jordan and heights of Hermon,
from the Mount of Mizar:

Deep calls to deep in the roar of your waterfalls.
All your waves and breakers are swept over me.

By day Adonai directs love
and at night the song within me
is a prayer to the God of my life.

I say to El my Rock, "why do you forget me?
Why must I go about mourning,
oppressed by enmity?"

With mortal agony in my bones,
taunted by adversity,
while all day they say to me,
"Where is your God?"

Why are you downcast, my soul?
Why are you disturbed within me?
Put hope in God, whom I will yet praise,
my saving help and God.

•

On the original Easter Sunday Jesus
breathed in, then onto them, and said, 'Receive
the holy breath, whose sins you forgive are forgiven…,'
breathing onto them and us the power to forgive. John 20.23

PSALM 43

Antiphon *Blessed are those mourning,
for they will be comforted.*   Mt 5:4

God, vindicate me;
plead my cause against an ungodly nation;
rescue me from humans deceitful doing the bad.

God, my strength, why am I rejected?
Why must I go about mourning,
oppressed by enmity?

Send forth your light and your fidelity;
let them guide me to your dwellings
and bring me to your holy mountain.

Then I will go to the altar of God,
to El, my joy and delight,
and I will praise you with harp, God, my God.

Why are you downcast, my soul?
Why are you disturbed within me?
Put hope in God, whom I will yet praise,
the saving help of my face, my God.

• • •

*Evangelization
is one beggar telling
another beggar where to
find bread.*   D.T. Niles

Day 9 - MORNING

PSALM 44

Antiphon *The reign of heaven is like leaven
a woman mixes into three measures
of flour until the whole is leavened.* Mt 13:33

With our ears, God, we have heard,
our ancestors told us the deed you did
in their days, in days long ago.

You drove out nations by your hand
and you planted them;
you crushed peoples so they could flourish.

For they won victory not by their sword and arm,
but by your right hand and arm
and the light of your faces,
for you loved them.

You are my Ruler and my God;
decree the victories of Jacob.
Through you we push back enmity;
through your name we trample opposition.

Indeed I trust not in my bow
and my sword does not bring me victory,
but you give to us victory over enmity
and shame the adversity.
In God we boast all the day
and we will praise your name to forever.

Day 9 - MORNING
Psalm 44, continued

But you let us be rejected and humbled
and you do not go out with our armies.
You turned us back before enmity
and adversity plundered from us.

You gave us up like sheep devoured;
among the nations you scattered us.
You sold your people for no great price,
gaining nothing from their sale.

You made us a reproach to our neighbors,
scorn and derision to those around us.
You made us a byword among the nations,
a shaking of heads among the peoples.

All the day my disgrace is before me
and shame covers my face
at taunts of reproachers and revilers
because of avenging enmity.

All of this though we did not forget you
and were not false to your covenant.
Our hearts did not turn back
and our feet did not stray from your path,
but you pushed us into haunts of jackals
and you covered us over with deep darkness.

Day 9 - MORNING

If we forgot the name of our God,
if we spread out our hands to a foreign "god,"
would God not have discovered this,
the One knowing the secrets of the heart?
Yet for you we face death all the day;
we are considered as sheep for slaughter.

Wake up, Lord! Why do you sleep?
Rouse yourself! Do not reject us to forever.
Why do you hide your faces
and forget our misery and oppression?

Indeed our self is brought down to the dust;
our body clings to the ground.
Rise up as our help and redeem us!
because of your unfailing love.

•

---

*A human has the right to act in conscience
and in freedom so as personally to make moral
decisions and 'must not be forced to act contrary to
their conscience. Nor must they be prevented from acting
according to their conscience, especially in religious matters.'*
See *Catechism* #1782, Vatican II *Declaration on Religious Freedom*

PSALM 45

Antiphon   *Rejoice on that day and leap for joy,
for great is your reward in heaven.*   Lk 6:23

My heart is stirred with a noble theme;
I recite my verses for the ruler;
my tongue is a pen of a skillful scribe.

You were anointed with grace on your lips,
more excellent among children of humanity.
For thus has God blessed you to forever.

Gird your sword upon your side, mighty one,
your splendor and your majesty.
Your majesty, be victorious!
Ride forth on behalf of truth and justice;
let your right hand display awesome deeds.

Your arrows are sharp;
let nations fall beneath you into the heart
of ones who choose enmity with the royal
on God's throne forever and ever.
The scepter of the realm is a scepter of justice.

You love justice
and hate when people do the bad;
for this your God anointed you
above your companions with oil of gladness,
with myrrh and aloes and cassia on your robes,
and from ivory palaces strings make you glad.

Day 9 - MORNING

Children of royalty are honored among you
and the royal spouse stands at your right hand,
honored in gold of Ophir.

Listen, child, and consider!
Give your ear and forget your people
and the house of your parents.
The ruler enthralled for your beauty
is your lord, so give honor!
With the gift of your face, child of Tyre,
wealthy people will seek you.

The all-glorious offspring of the ruler
is in a gown with interweavings of gold,
led to the ruler in embroidered garments
with virgin companions following.
They are led in with joy and gladness;
they enter the royal palace.

In the place of your parents will your children be,
as royals through all the land.
I will make perpetual the memory of your name
through all generations and generation.
For this the nations will praise you
ever and to forever.

•

Nothing in life is to be feared, it is only to be understood.
Now is the time to understand more, so that we may fear less.
Maria Sktodowska-Curie

PSALM 46

Antiphon — *Do you want to be whole?* — Jn 5:6

God is our refuge and strength,
our help in troubles, ever present.
And so we will not fear,
even if earth were to give way,
even if mountains were to fall
into the heart of the sea,
even if sea waters foam
or mountains quake with their surging.

River streams make glad the city of God,
the holy dwelling place of the Most High.
God is inside her and she will not fall.
God will help her at break of day.
Nations are in uproar and realms fall;
the earth melts at the voice of God.

Adonai Sabaoth is with us;
the God of Jacob is our fortress.

Come and see the works of Adonai,
the desolations brought on the earth:
making wars to cease to the ends of the earth,
breaking the bow and shattering the spear
and burning with fire the chariot and shield.

Day 9 - MORNING

"Be still! And know that I am God.
I will be exalted among the nations;
I will be exalted on the earth."

Adonai Sabaoth is with us;
the God of Jacob is our fortress.

• • •

O God,
lead all who plan and conduct business to wise and honest decisions
and give them the grace to carry them out fairly for the common good.
Like the Carpenter, may all who skillfully transform the things you have
created know their dignity and be fulfilled in making human lives better.
And may buyers and sellers embody justice and charity
and find joy in the progress of the whole earthly city.

Workers in Offices, Shops & Markets
adapted from the *Book of Blessings*

PSALM 47

Antiphon *Behold, I am with you all the days*
until the completion of the eon.   Mt 28:20

All you nations, clap your hands!
Shout to God with cries of joy!
How awesome, Most High Adonai.

The great Ruler over all the earth
subdued nations under us
and peoples under our feet,
and chose for us an inheritance,
the pride of Jacob the beloved.

God ascended with shouts of joy,
Adonai amid sound of trumpet.
Sing praises to God, sing praises.
Sing praises to our Ruler, sing praises.

For God, Ruler of all the earth, sing praises.
God reigns over the nations,
God sits on the holy throne.

Nobles of nations assemble
with the people of the God of Abraham.
The shields of the earth belong to God
who is greatly exalted.

•

PSALM 48

Antiphon *Take nothing on the way*
except a staff, sandals,
and a single tunic. Mk 6:8

Great is Adonai, greatly being praised
in the city of our God, on the holy mountain,
beautiful height, the joy of all the earth,

Mount Zion, the upmost heights,
sacred mountain, the city of the Great Ruler.
God in the citadels is shown as a fortress when,
see, the rulers join forces and invade together.

They saw, were astounded, and fled in terror;
trembling seized them, pain
like a woman in labor.
By the east wind you destroyed
ships of Tarshish;

just as we heard, so we saw in the city
of Adonai Sabaoth, in the city of our God.
God makes her secure to forever.

In your temple we meditate
on your unfailing love.
Like your name, God, so your praise
goes to the ends of the earth;

Psalm 48, continued

your right hand is filled with justice.
Mount Zion rejoices
because of your judgments;
the villages of Judah are glad.

Walk about Zion! Go all around!
Count her towers!
Consider at heart her ramparts!
View her citadels!
So that you may tell to the next generation:
This God, our God, forever and ever
will guide us to the always.

•

---

*Emperor
Constantine's
Edict of Milan in
313 AD diminished
the general risk of being
a martyr, which had been
seen by many as the highest
form of Christian life. And so
some sought to pattern their lives
after Jesus' 40 days of temptation in
the desert, but in desert caves in Egypt
and Syria praying primarily the psalms. Over
time others began to live in nearby caves seeking
spiritual direction from the one they would treat as
a kind of father or abba, such as Saint Anthony of Egypt.*

PSALM 49

Antiphon   *You cannot serve God and mammon;*
where your treasure is
there also will your heart be.   Mt 6:24b,21

Hear this all peoples! Listen, all alive in the world!
Men and women, all sons and daughters,
rich and poor alike:

My mouth will speak words of wisdom
and my heart utter understanding of things.
I will turn an ear to a proverb;
I will expound my riddle with harp music.

Why should I fear in days of the bad
the deceivers who surround me,
the trusters of wealth,
and the boasters of the greatness of their riches?

No human can redeem redemption of another,
nor for oneself give a ransom to God.
Ransom of a life is costly; no ransom can be enough
for one to live to forever and not see the decay.

For we see that even wise people die;
like the foolish and the senseless they perish,
and leave all their wealth to others.

Psalm 49, continued

Their thoughts are of their houses to forever
as their dwelling for generations and generation,
and so they call lands by their own names.

The human, despite riches, does not endure,
but perishes just like the beasts.

This is their fate who trust in themselves
and their followers who give them approval.
Like the sheep they are destined for Sheol,
and death will be their shepherd.

Upright ones will rule over them in the morning
and their form will decay in Sheol, their mansion.
But God will redeem my soul
and take me from the hand of Sheol.

Be not overawed when human beings grow rich,
when they increase the splendor of their houses.
For in death they will take none of it;
with none of their splendor will they descend.

Though during their lives they blessed themselves,
and people do praise you when you prosper,
they will go to the generation of their ancestors
and never see light to forever.

Like the beast that must perish
so is a human with riches
but still poor in understanding.

• • •

Day 10 - MORNING

PSALM 50

Antiphon   *I desire mercy and not sacrifice,*
knowledge of God
rather than burnt offerings.   Mt 9:13a; 12:7;
Hosea 6:6

El Elohim Adonai
speaks and summons earth
from the rising of the sun to its setting.
From Zion, perfect of beauty, God shines forth.

Our God comes and will not be silent,
before whom a fire devours,
around whom a storm is fierce.
The heavens at above are summoned,
and the earth to judge the people:

"Gather the ones faithful to me,
the ones making my covenant by sacrifice."
The heavens proclaim the justice of God,
the One who is judge.

"Hear, my people, and I will speak, Israel,
and I will testify against you;
God, your God, am I.

Not for your sacrifices do I rebuke you,
or your burnt offerings ever before me.
I do not need a bull from your stall
or goats from your pen,

Day 10 - MORNING
Psalm 50, continued

for every animal of the forest is mine,
cattle on the mountains, the thousands.
I know every bird in the air,
and every creature of fields is mine.

Were I hungry, I would not tell it to you,
for the world is mine and all in her.
Do I eat the flesh of bulls?
Drink the blood of goats?

Offer thanksgiving as your sacrifice to God!
And fulfill your vows to the Most High!
Call upon me in the day of trouble;
I will deliver you and you will honor me."

But God says to those who do the bad,
"What to you to recite my laws
or to take my covenant on your lips?
You hate instruction,
and cast my words behind you.

When you see a thief, you join in,
and cast your lot with doers of adultery.
You use your mouth for the bad
and harness your tongue to deceit.

You sit and speak against your brother and sister
and slander your mother's children.
You did these, and I kept silent;
you thought me to be like you?

Day 10 - MORNING

...Consider now this: ...there is no one to rescue
...those who insist on forgetting God.
One offering thanksgiving offered as a sacrifice,
I will show that one to the salvation of God."

•

It is quite possible for a human
to have none but the purest thoughts
and yet be so distracted mulling over them
that one remains the while far removed from God.

See *Chapters on Prayer* (#55) by Evagrius Ponticus

PSALM 51

Antiphon *If anyone serves me,*
that one the Abba will honor. Jn 12:26b

Have mercy on me, God,
in accord with your unfailing love;
in accord with your great compassion
blot out my transgressions.

Wash me of my many iniquities
and cleanse me from my sin,
for I know my transgressions
and my sin is before me always.

Against you yourself I sinned,
doing what is bad in your eyes.
You are proven right when you speak
and justified when you judge.
Surely we are sinners from birth,
from conception in a mother's womb.

Surely you desire truth in our inner parts;
in my inmost place you teach me wisdom.
You cleanse me with hyssop and I will be clean;
you wash me and I will be whiter than snow…

You let me hear joy and gladness;
let the bones you let be crushed now rejoice.
Hide your faces from my sins
and blot out all my iniquities.

Day 10 - MORNING

A clean heart create in me, God!
Renew inside me a spirit to be steadfast.
Do not cast me from your presences,
nor take from me your Holy Spirit.

Restore to me the joy of your salvation
and sustain in me a willing spirit.
I will teach transgressors your ways
and sinners will turn back to you.

Save me from bloodguilt, God,
God of my salvation;
my tongue will sing of your justice.
Lord, open my lips
and my mouth will proclaim your praise.

Sacrifices give you no delight;
I could bring a burnt offering,
but it would give you no pleasure.
The sacrifices, God, you will not despise
are a broken spirit and a contrite heart.

Make Zion prosper in your pleasure,
and build up the walls of Jerusalem.
Then you will delight in the sacrifice of the just,
burnt offerings and whole offerings,
bulls offered on your altar.

•

PSALM 52

Antiphon *Laying his hands
on each one brought to him,
Jesus healed those ailing with disease.*   Lk 4:40b

Why, mighty liar, do you boast of the bad
to the disgrace of El all the day?
Your tongue plots destruction
like a sharpened razor, practicing deceit.

You love the bad rather than the good,
lies rather than honest speech.
Your tongue of deceit loves every harmful word.

Surely El will bring you down,
snatch you from your tent,
and uproot you from the land of the living.

Then the just will see and fear,
and they will laugh at you.
See the one who did not see God as the refuge,
but grew strong by destruction
and trusted in great wealth.

But I am like an olive tree
flourishing in the house of God;
I trust in God's unfailing love forever and ever.

I will praise you to forever
for what you have done,
and in the presence of your saints
I will hope in you
for your name is good.

• • •

PSALM 53

Antiphon *Whoever does not receive the reign of God as a child by no means may enter into it.*   Mk 10:15

In the heart of a fool is said, "There is no God."
The bad way is vile and corrupt;
there is no one doing good.

God looks from the heavens
on children of humanity
to see if there is one who understands,
one who is seeking God.

All of them turned away together;
they became corrupt;
there is no one doing good, not even one.

Will the ones doing the bad never learn?
Devouring my people, they eat bread;
they do not call on God.

There they dreaded as dread had not been,
for God scattered the bones of attackers
put to shame in God's rejection.

Who would be brought from Zion
for the salvation of Israel?
When God restores the people of God,
let Jacob rejoice, let Israel be glad.

●

PSALM 54:1-6,8-9

Antiphon *The Son of Humanity will be betrayed
into human hands and they will kill him,
and three days after being killed
he will rise up.*   Mk 9:31

God, save me by your name
and by your might vindicate me.
God, hear my prayer!
Listen to the words of my mouth!

For strangers attack me
and ruthless people seek my life
without regard for God before them.
See, God is helping me!
The Lord sustains my self…

With a freewill offering I will sacrifice to you;
I will praise, Adonai, your good name,
for my eyes have seen enmity
but you delivered me from every trouble.

•

---

*The opposite of war
isn't peace…; it's creation.*
Jonathan Larson, d. 1996, composer/playwright

PSALM 55:2-15,17-24

Antiphon *Whoever receives me
receives the One who sent me.*   Mk 9:37b

Listen, Elohim, to my prayer!
Ignore not my plea, but hear me and answer me,
as I am troubled by my thoughts
and groan at the voice of enmity,
at the stares of the faces of doers of the bad,
for they bring suffering down upon me
and revile me in anger.

My heart is in anguish within me
and the terrors of death assail me.
Fear and trembling harass me
and horror has overwhelmed me.

And I said, "If I had wings like the dove;
I would fly away and find rest.
See! I would flee far and stay in the desert.
I would hurry to my place of shelter
from the storm of the raging wind."

Confuse them, Lord; confound their scheming,
for I see violence and strife in the city.
By day and by night they prowl on her walls;
within her are malice and abuse.

Destructive forces are within her
and threats and lies never leave her streets. -

Day 10 - EVENING

It is not insults of enmity rising against me;
from that I could hide and endure.

But it is you, my other self, my companion,
my friend with whom together
we shared close companionship
walking with the throng at the house of Elohim...

To Elohim I call and am saved by Adonai
who hears my voice when I cry out in distress
at dusk, dawn and noon,
who ransoms my whole self from battle
though many oppose me.

El enthroned forever will hear and let be afflicted
those who never allow themselves to change,
who have no fear of God,
who stretch hands against friends,
and violate covenants.

This one's mouth is smooth as butter,
yet war is in the heart,
speaking words more soothing than oil
that are yet drawn swords.

Cast your cares on Adonai, who will sustain you
and to forever let not the just fall.

But you, God, will bring bloody deceit
into the pit of corruption,
not living half their days;
And I will trust in you.

• • •

PSALM 56:2-7,9-14

Antiphon *The word of God is the seed.* Lk 8:11b

Be merciful to me, my God!
Human beings pursue me all the day,
attacking with oppression
and with slander all the day.

Indeed in their pride do the many attack me.
On the day I am afraid, in you I trust.
My praise is of God's word, in God I trust.
I will not be afraid; what can a mortal do to me?

All the day they twist my words against me;
all their plots are for harm.
They conspire, they lurk, they watch my steps;
they are eager for my life…

Record my lament, put my tears in your wineskin;
are they not in your record?
Enmity will turn back on the day I call;

I will know that God is for me.
In God whose word I praise,
in Adonai whose word I praise, in God I trust.
I will not be afraid; what can a human do to me?

Upon me, God, are my vows to you;
I will present thank offerings to you
for you delivered my soul from death
and my feet from stumbling,
to walk in God's presence
in the light of the living.

PSALM 57

Antiphon

*This is my comandment,
that you love one another
as I have loved you.* Jn 15:12

Have mercy on me, **God**, have mercy on me,
for in you my soul takes refuge
and in the shade of your wings I take refuge
until disasters pass.

I cry out to God Most High,
to El who fulfills me,
who sends from the heavens and saves me
and rebukes the one pursuing me.

God sends love and fidelity to my self;
in the midst of ravenous lions I lie,
in the midst of human beings
with teeth and spear and arrows and tongues,
their sharp swords.

Be exalted, God, above the heavens,
your glory over all the earth.

For my feet they spread a net
and my self was bowed down.
Before me they dug a pit
and fell inside it themselves.

Day 11 - MORNING

My heart is steadfast, Elohim,
my heart is steadfast;
I will sing and make music.

Awake, my soul!
Wake up the harp and the lyre;
I will wake up the dawn.

I will praise you among the nations, Lord;
I will sing of you among the peoples,
for great to the heavens is your love
and to the skies is your fidelity.

Be exalted above the heavens, God,
your glory over all the earth.

• • •

Note: Psalm 58 is omitted
in the *Liturgy of the Hours*

You feel
you are hedged
in; you dream of escape;
but beware of mirages. Do not
run or fly away in order to get free:
rather dig in the narrow place which has
been given you; you will find God there and
everything. God does not float on your horizon,
but sleeps in your substance. Vanity runs, love digs.
If you fly away from yourself, your prison will run with
you and will close in because of the wind of your flight; if
you go deep down into yourself it will disappear in paradise.

See *Homo Viator (Human Wayfarer)* by Gabriel Marcel

PSALM 59:2-5,10-11a,17-18

Antiphon *The reign of heaven is like
a merchant who seeking fine pearls
finds one precious pearl and going away
sells everything and buys it.*   Mt 13:45,46

Deliver me from enmity; protect me, God,
from those who rise up against me.
Deliver me from doers of the bad
and save me from bloody ways.

See, they lie in wait for my self;
fierce people conspire against me
for no offense of me nor sin, Adonai.
For no wrong they make ready to attack;
arise to help me and look!...

For you, my Strength, I watch,
for you God, my fortress,
you God are my love.

I will sing of your strength
and I will sing at dawn of your love,
for you are my fortress
and my refuge in times of trouble.

To you, my Strength, I sing praise
for you God, my fortress,
you God are my love.

•

Day 11 - EVENING

PSALM 60:3-14a

Antiphon   *Do not judge,*
           lest you be judged.   Mt 7:1

God you rejected us,
breaking our defenses;
you were angry, now restore us.

You shook the land and tore her open;
mend her fractures, for she quakes!
You showed your people a desperate time;
you made us drink wine to staggering.

For those who fear you, you raised a banner
to be unfurled against the bow,
that your beloved ones may be delivered.
Help us with your right hand and save us!

God spoke from the sanctuary:
"I will triumph and parcel out Shechem,
and measure out the valley of Succoth;
mine are Gilead and Manasseh,

Ephraim my head helmet,
Judah my scepter,
and Moab my washbasin;
On Edom I toss my sandal
and over Philistia I shout in triumph"

Psalm 60, continued

Who will bring me to the Fortress City?
Who will lead me to Edom?
Have you, God, not rejected us,
and not gone out, God, with our armies?

Against enmity give to us aid,
for worthless is human help.
In God will we gain the victory…

•

> *I can never really know what goes on
> in the heart of another. Indeed I hardly
> know what is going on in my own heart,
> but God knows. Only God has all the data,
> and so the job of judging belongs to God alone.*

PSALM 61

Antiphon
*Come to me,
all who labor and are burdened,
and I will rest you;
my yoke is gentle
and my burden is light.*   Mt 11:28,30

Hear, God, my cry! Listen to my prayer!
From the edge of the earth I call to you
as my heart grows faint.

To the high rock you lead me
for you are my refuge
and tower of strength against adversity.

I would dwell in your tent for forevers
and take refuge in the shelter of your wings.
For you, God, hearing my vows,
gave inheritance to those revering your name.

You increase the days upon days of the royal one,
and the years for generation and generation,
enthroned in God's presences forever,
appointed and protected in God's love and fidelity.

I will sing praise of your name forever
to fulfill my vows day by day.

• • •

PSALM 62

Antiphon *Do not worry about tomorrow
for tomorrow will worry about itself;
sufficient to the day is its own trouble.* Mt 6:34

My soul finds rest in God alone,
from whom is my salvation,
alone my salvation and my rock,
my fortress never to be shaken.

Until when will you assault a human being,
will you throw down, all of you,
like a leaning wall or a tottering fence?

They fully intend to topple from the lofty place;
they delight in lies
and bless with their mouth
and curse in their heart.

My soul finds rest in God alone,
from whom is my hope,
alone my salvation and my rock,
my fortress not to be shaken.

From God is my salvation and my honor;
my mighty rock and refuge.
Trust in God at all times, people;
pour out your heart to God our refuge.

Sons and daughters of humanity are but a breath;
the so-called great ones are an illusion.
On balanced scales they both rise;
together they are only a breath.

Trust not in extortion
and take no pride in stolen things;
even when riches increase
do not set your heart on them.

One thing God has spoken,
two things I have heard:
that to God is power
and to you, Lord, is love;
and surely you will reward to each
according to our deeds.

•

---

*To be grateful is to recognize the love of
God in everything God has given us – and
God has given us everything. Every breath
we draw is a gift of God's love, every moment
of existence is a grace, for it brings with it immense
graces from God. Gratitude therefore takes nothing for
granted, is never unresponsive, is constantly awakening
to new wonder and to praise of the goodness of God. For
the grateful human know that God is good, not by hearsay
but by experience. And that is what makes all the difference.*

See *Thoughts in Solitude* by Thomas Merton

PSALM 63:1-8

Antiphon *Watch ready, for you know
neither the day nor the hour.* Mt 25:13

God, you are my God; you I earnestly seek.
My soul, she thirsts for you,
my body, he longs for you,
as in a land with no water, dry and weary.

So in the sanctuary I saw you,
beheld you in your power and glory.
Your love is better than life itself;
my lips will glorify you.

So I will praise you in all the ways I am alive;
calling your name I will lift up my hands.
As with fatness and richness,
my soul will be satisfied;
with singing lips my mouth will sing praise.

When I remember you on my bed,
through night watches I think of you,
you who are my help;
then in the shadow of your wings I sing.
My very self stays close to you;
your right hand upholds me.

●

Day 12 - MORNING

PSALM 64

Antiphon   *Abba, forgive them,*
           for they know not what they do.   Lk 23:34

Hear my voice, O God, in complaint;
threatened by enmity, you protect my life.
You hide me from conspiracies,
from the noisy crowd of people doing bad things,

who sharpen their tongue like the sword,
aim their arrow of harmful words,
and shoot from ambush the innocent person;
they shoot suddenly and without fear.

They encourage those who plan harm,
and they talk of hidden snares,
saying, "who will see them?"
They plot injustices they call "the perfect plan!"
Surely the human mind and heart are cunning.

But God will shoot sudden arrows
striking down those plans.
Their ruin will be by their own tongues;
all who see them will shake heads at them.

All humanity will fear,
then come to proclaim the work of God,
and ponder the deeds of God.
Let the just rejoice and take refuge in Adonai;
let all the upright of heart give praise.

• • •

PSALM 65

Antiphon   *And that sown on the good soil*
is the one hearing
and understanding the word,
who indeed bears fruit.   Mt 13:23

For you, **O God**, praise we owe in Zion,
and to you will our vow be fulfilled.

You hear our prayer.
To you all humanity will come.
When my sins overwhelm me
you forgive them.

Blessed are the ones you choose
and bring near to live in your courts.
We are filled with the goodness of your house
and the holiness of your temple.

Deeds awesome and just are your answer,
God of our salvation,
hope of all the ends of the earth
and of the far seas.

You form mountains by your power,
arming yourself with strength.
You still the roar of the seas,
the roar of their waves,
and the turmoil of nations.

Those who live in far away places
fear your wonders;
in dawns of morning and in the evening
you call forth songs of joy.

You care for the land and water her;
with an abundance you enrich her.
God's stream is as you ordain the earth:
filled with waters, providing grain.
You drench its furrows and level its ridges;
you soften her with showers and bless the crops.

You crown the year with your bounty;
paths overflow with your abundance.
The desert grasslands are overflowing
and the hills are clothed with gladness.

The meadows are covered with the flock
and valleys are coated with grain.
They shout for joy; for joy they sing.

•

You do not have to change for God to love you.

Be grateful for your sins; they are carriers of grace.

Say goodbye to golden yesterdays
or your heart will never learn to love the present.

Anthoney de Mello, Jesuit
See *Hearts on Fire: Praying with Jesuits* by Michael Harter, S.J.

PSALM 66

Antiphon *The harvest is plenty but workers are few;*
ask the Lord of the harvest
to cast workers into the harvest.   Lk 10:2

Shout joy to God all you earth!
Sing the glory of the name!
Offer glory and praise to God!
Say to God, "How awesome are you;
how great are your deeds."

Enmity cringes before you and your power.
All of the earth bow down to you,
they sing praise to you,
they sing praise to your name.

Come and see the deeds of God who is awesome,
the works on behalf of all sons and daughters.
God turned the sea into dry land;
through the river they passed on foot.

Let us rejoice in God,
who rules forever with power
with eyes watching the nations.
Let no rebels rise up.

Peoples, make heard the praise of our God
who preserves our life among the living,
and lets not our feet to slip.

God, you tested us, refined us as silver is refined.
You let us be brought into prison,
you let burdens be put on our backs,
you let human beings set foot on our neck.

We went through the fire and through the waters
and you brought us to a spacious place.

I will come to your temple with burnt offerings,
I will fulfill to you my vows, promised on my lips,
spoken in a time of trouble.

Sacrifices of fat animals I will sacrifice to you;
with offerings of rams I will offer bull and goats.

Come! Listen! Let me tell all who fear God
what God has done for my very self.
To God my mouth cried out
with praise on my tongue.

If I cherished sin in my heart
the Lord would not have listened.
Surely God listened and heard my voice of prayer.

God, be praised, who rejected not my prayer
nor took from within me
the Lord's own *hesed* love.

•

In a culture of vocations, all of us would be helping each other discern what God's call is for our life, this year, this day.

PSALM 67

Antiphon *Peace I leave with you;*
my peace I give to you. Jn 14:27a

May God be gracious to us and bless us,
may God's faces shine upon us.
How else can your ways be known on the earth
and your salvation among all the nations?

May the peoples praise you, God,
may the peoples praise you, all of them.

May the nations be glad and sing for joy
for you rule the peoples
and guide nations of the earth into justice.

May the peoples praise you, God,
may the peoples praise you, all of them.

The land will yield her harvest, God will bless us,
and all the ends of the earth will revere our God.

• • •

Can we speak of the Christian as a
musical instrument played by the Holy Spirit?
Saint Gregory Nazianzen

Day 13 - MORNING

PSALM 68

Antiphon　*When you are invited, take the lowest place;*
one exalting the self will be humbled,
and one humbling the self will be exalted.
Lk 14:10,11

May God arise
and may enmity flee and be scattered.
As smoke is blown, let it blow;
as wax melts before fire
may bad ways perish from before God.

But may just ones be glad
and rejoice before God;
may they be happy with joy.
Sing to God! Sing praise to the name!
Extol the Rider of the Clouds,
and rejoice in the name Adonai,

Abba of the fatherless
and defender of widows,
God dwelling in holiness.
God sets the lonely into a family
and leads prisoners forth with songs,
but ones rebelling live on sun-scorched land.

Psalm 68, continued

When you went out before your people, God,
when you marched through the wasteland,
the earth shook and heavens poured rain
before the One God of Sinai,
before God, the God of Israel.

You gave a shower of abundances, God,
on your inheritance;
even the weary you refreshed.
Your people settled in her, God;
you provided for the poor from your bounty.

The Lord announced the word,
a great company of proclaimers.
Rulers and armies flee, they flee,
and in resident camps the plunder is divided.

While you sleep among campfires
wings of dove are sheathed with silver
and her feathers with the shine of gold.
When Shaddai scatters the rulers,
the scattering is like snow on Zalmon.

A majestic mountain, the mountain of Bashan,
a rugged mountain is the mountain of Bashan.
Why gaze in envy, you rugged mountains,
at the mountain God chooses for the reign,
indeed where Adonai will dwell to forever?

Chariots of God are tens of thousands,
thousands of the multitude
into the Sinai sanctuary.
You ascended to the height and led captive;
you received gifts from human beings,
and even from those rebelling,
to your dwelling, God Adonai.

The Lord is being praised day by day,
bearing our burden is El our Savior.
Our El, the El of salvation,
the Lord Adonai is the escape from death.
Surely God will silence the plans of enmity,
in the crown of their hair where sins go on.

The Lord says, "From Bashan I will bring,
I will bring from depths of the sea,
that you may wash your foot in their defeat
and the tongues of your dogs have their share."

They view your processions, God,
processions into the sanctuary
of my God and my Ruler.
Singers are in front, followed by musicians
among girls playing tambourines.

In great congregations, praise God;
praise Adonai in the assembly of Israel!
There little Benjamin leads the royals of Judah,
their throng the royals of Zebulun and Naphtali.

Day 13 - MORNING
Psalm 68, continued

You, God, summoned your power.
Show strength, God, as you did for us!
Because of your temple at Jerusalem,
to you the rulers will bring gifts.

Rebuke the beast of the reeds,
the herd of bulls among calves of nations;
being humbled with bars of silver,
nations that delight in wars are scattered.
Envoys from Egypt will come;
Ethiopia will submit their hands to God.

Peoples of the earth, sing to God!
Sing praise to the Lord, the Rider in the skies,
the ancient heavens, see!
The voice thunders, the voice of might.

Proclaim the power of God over Israel,
the majesty and power in the skies.
Awesome are you, God, in your sanctuary;
the God of Israel gives power and strengths
to the people praising God.

• • •

If fear must be my primary or
only motivator, then let my fear be only
of God, whose Son has told us to 'be not afraid.'

Day 13 - EVENING

PSALM 69:2-22,30-37

Antiphon *Be not afraid of ones who can kill the body
but are unable to kill the soul;
fear only the One able to destroy
both soul and body in gehenna.* Mt 10:28

Save me, Adonai,
for waters have come to my neck.

I sink into the deep mire; there is no foothold.
I have come into deep waters; floods engulf me.

I am worn out from calling out;
my throat is parched and my eyes fail,
looking for my God.

Those hating me for no reason
are more numerous than the hairs of my head.
Many are the ones destroying me
in enmity for no reason.

What I did not steal, must I now restore?
You, God, you know my folly
and my guilts are not hidden from you.

May those who hope in you, God of Israel,
not be disgraced because of me.
For your sake I endure scorn
and shame covers my face.

Psalm 69, continued

I am a stranger to my brothers and sisters,
an alien to the children of my mother.
Zeal for your house consumes me
and insults of your insulters fall on me.

When I weep and fast, my self is a scorn to me.
When I put on my clothing of sackcloth
then I am as sport to them.
Those sitting at the gate mock at me
and drinkers of strong drink in their songs.

But I pray to you, Adonai, in the time of favor;
in the greatness of your love, God,
answer me with your sure salvation.

Rescue me from the mire and let me not sink;
let me be delivered from those who hate
and from the depths of the waters.
Let not the flood of waters engulf me,
nor the deep swallow me
nor the pit close its mouth over me.

Answer me, Adonai, for good is your love!
In your great mercies, turn to me!
Hide not your faces from your servant;
to my trouble, be quick! Answer me!
Come near because of the adversity;
rescue my self and redeem me!

You know my scorn and shame and disgrace;
all in enmity stand before you.
Scorn broke my heart and I became helpless
and I looked for compassion but there was none,
and for comforters, but found none.

They put gall in my food
and for my thirst gave me vinegar to drink…
I am in pain and suffering;
may your salvation protect me, God.

I will praise God's name in song and glory
with a thanksgiving more pleasing to Adonai
than ox or bull with horn and hoof.

The poor ones will see and be glad;
may your hearts now live, you seekers of God,
for Adonai hears the needy ones
and despises not the captives.

Let heaven and earth give praise
with the seas and all moving in them.
For God will save Zion
and rebuild the cities of Judah;

then they will settle there and be her steward
and the children of the servants will inherit her
and lovers of the Name will dwell in her.

●

PSALM 70

Antiphon *You have heard it said,*
an eye for an eye and a tooth for a tooth;
but I say to you, do not resist a doer of bad;
when someone strikes you on the right cheek,
give the other as well. Mt 5:38,39

God, come to save me;
Adonai, make haste to help me!
May plans to seek my life
be shamed and confused;

may the desire for my ruin
be turned back in disgrace
and ones saying "aha!, aha!"
turn back in shame.

May all who seek you
rejoice in you and be glad
and may lovers of salvation say always,
"Let God be exalted."

Yet I am poor and needy, God,
come quickly to me and do not delay,
Adonai, my help and deliverer.

• • •

An eye for an eye makes the whole world blind.
attributed to Gandhi

Day 14 - MORNING

PSALM 71

Antiphon
*Amen I tell you
that no prophet is acceptable
in their native place.* Lk 4:24

In you, Adonai, I take refuge;
to forever, let me not be shamed.
In your justice you rescue and deliver me.
Turn your ear to me and save me!

Be to me as a rock, and a refuge to go to always.
Command that I be saved,
for you are my rock and my fortress.
My God, deliver me
from the hands and from the grasp
of doers of the cruel bad,

for you are my hope, Lord Adonai,
my confidence since my youth.
I have relied on you from birth,
from my mother's womb you brought me forth;
my praise is ever to you.

To many I became like a portent
but you are my strong refuge.
My mouth is filled all the day
with praise of your splendor.
Cast me not away at my time of old age;
forsake me not when my strength is gone.

Psalm 71, continued

Enmity speaks against me;
waiting on my life, conspirers together say,
"God has forsaken that one! Pursue to seize,
for no one is coming to the rescue!"

God, be not far from me.
God, come quickly to help me!
May accusations against me perish in shame.
May scorn and disgrace
cover the desire to do harm.

But I will hope always and add praise of you.
My mouth will tell of your just deeds,
all the day of your salvation,
though I know not its measure;

I will come in mighty acts of Lord Adonai;
I will tell of your singular justice.
You taught me, God, since my youth;
to this day I declare your marvelous deeds.

Even in my old age and gray hair
you do not forsake me, God,
till I delcare your power to this generation,
your might to all yet to come,
and your justice to the heavens,
you, God, who have done great things.
Who, God, is equal to you?

Day 14 - MORNING

Though you let me see troubles, many and bitter,
you will again let me live.
And from the depths of the earth
you will again raise me up.
You will restore my honor
and you will again comfort me.

With the harp instrument I will praise you
and your faithfulness, my God;
I will sing praise to you with lyre,
Holy One of Israel.

My lips will shout for joy
when I sing praise to you,
even my self whom you redeemed.

Also my tongue will tell
all the day of your justice,
for desires of some to harm me
are in shame and confusion.

•

Psalm 71
is known as a
song of the elders.

PSALM 72

Antiphon *Out of you, Bethlehem, will come forth a ruler*
who will shepherd my people Israel. Mt 2:6;
Micah 5:2

God, endow your justice to King Solomon
and your judgment to the royal heir,
to judge your people with integrity
and your afflicted with justice.

Mountains will bring prosperity to the people,
the hills too in abundance.
He is to defend people afflicted,
save the children of the needy,
and crush the oppressor.

They will fear you as long as the sun,
as long as the moon,
from generation to generations.
He is to be like rain falling on a mown field,
like showers watering the earth.

In his days the just are to flourish
in prosperous abundance til the moon is no more.
He will rule from sea to sea
and from the River to the ends of the earth.

Desert tribes will bow;
the royals of Tarshish and the distant shores   --

Day 14 - MORNING

will bring tribute and present gifts
with royals of Sheba and Seba.
They will bow down to him;
the royals of all the nations will thus serve.

For he is to deliver the needy one crying out
and the afflicted one when no one is helping,
to take pity on the weak and the needy
and save the lives of the poor;

to rescue their lives
from oppression and violence,
for their lifeblood will be precious in his eyes.

May he live and be given gold of Sheba;
may all ever pray that he be blessed all the day.

May grain be abundant throughout the land,
on tops of hills, swaying like the fruit of Lebanon,
and people flourish and thrive like grass in a field.

May his name endure to forever
and continue as long as the sun;
being thus blessed, may the nations bless him.

Blessed be God, Adonai, God of Israel,
alone doing marvelous deeds.
Blessed be the glory of the name to forever;
may the earth be filled with the glory of God.
Amen and amen.

• • •

PSALM 73

Antiphon   *Any of you who do not detach*
from all your possessions
cannot be my disciple.   Lk 14:33

Surely good to Israel is El,
to those pure of heart.
But my feet almost slipped,
as nearly lost were my footholds,
for I envied the arrogant
and the prosperity of doers of the bad.

None of them struggle with death
and healthy are their bodies.
Human burdens are not theirs,
nor human plagues.

And so pride wraps them as a necklace
clothing violence on them.
Their eyes bulge with fat;
their conceits pass the limits of the mind.

They scoff and they speak with malice
and threaten arrogant oppression.
Their mouths lay claim to the heavens,
and their tongues to possession of the earth.

Day 14 - EVENING

And so people turn to them for themselves
as they drink all the waters of abundance.
They say, "How does El know?"
and, "Does the Most High know about this?"
See these doers of the bad:
even carefree of Always they increase their wealth.

Surely in vain have I kept my heart clean
and washed my hands in innocence.
But I am plagued all the day
and punished in the mornings.

If I said that I would speak as they do,
see the generation of your children I would betray!

My efforts to understand this
are oppressive to my eyes.
Until! I entered into sanctuaries of God
and understood about their final destiny.

Surely you place them on slippery ground
and cast them down to ruins.
How sudden is their destruction,
swept away complete by terrors.
As with a dream when waking up, Lord,
their fantasy you will despise when you arise.

When my heart was grieved,
and my spirits bitter
and senseless and unknowing,
I was but a brute beast before you.

Psalm 73, continued

Yet I am always with you;
you hold me by my right hand.
With your counsel you guide me
and will take me after the glory.

Who in the heavens is to me?
And with you, nothing on earth do I desire.
My flesh and my heart may fail,
but Elohim is the strength of my heart
and my portion to forever.

For see! Those far from you will perish…
But the nearness of Elohim is my good.
I have made you my refuge, Lord Adonai,
to tell of all your deeds.

●

---

*If we had any
possessions, we
should need weapons
and laws to defend them.*

Saint Francis of Assisi, d. 1221

PSALM 74

Antiphon *The Son of Humanity*
took our infirmities
and bore our diseases.   Mt 8:17
Isaiah 53:4

Why, God, do you reject us to forever?
Your anger smolders
against sheep of your pasture.
Remember your people you gathered of old,
your tribe of heirs you redeemed,
Mount Zion where you dwelt.

Lift high your steps through everlasting ruin,
the enmity destruction to the sanctuary.
Enmity roared in your meeting place
and set up their standard signs.

They behaved like ones raising axes
through a thicket of trees,
and now her carved panels
they smashed with axe and hatchet.
They sent your sanctuary to the ground with fire
and defiled the dwelling place of your Name.

Psalm 74, continued

They said in their heart, "We will crush them."
Completely they burned in the land
all the places to worship God.
We see no miraculous signs;
there is no longer a prophet among us.
Until when? No one knows.

Until when, God,
will enmity mock and revile your name?
To forever?
Why do you hold back your hand,
even your right hand
from the fold of your bosom?

But God, my Ruler from of old,
bringing salvation onto the midst of the earth,
you split open the sea by your power,
you break the heads of dragons in the waters.

You crushed the heads of Leviathan,
giving him as food
to people and desert creatures.
You opened up streams and springs
and dried up everflowing rivers.

To you is the day and to you is the night,
and you established the moon and the sun.
You set all the boundaries of the earth;
summer and winter were made by you.

Day 14 - EVENING

Remember how enmity mocks Adonai,
and foolish people revile your name.
Do not hand over to the wild beast
the life of your dove;
remember to forever
the life of your afflicted ones.

Scary places of the land
are haunted with violence.
So have regard for your covenant.
Let not the oppressed retreat, nor the disgraced;
may the poor and the needy praise your name.

Rise up, God! Defend your cause!
Remember the all-day mockery of fools.
Ignore not the clamor of enmity
nor those in continual uproar.

• • •

---

*Lamentations are part of many of the psalms,
but perhaps the most used little psalm of
lamentation has but one word, 'shit!'*

PSALM 75

Antiphon* *Let the one of you without sin
be the first to throw a stone.* Jn 8:7

*One
adulterer
is there, the
other is not. A mob
of self-appointed judges
demands judgment. After
the words of the just judge, all
the stones drop to the earth, one by one,
beginning with the eldest, presumed to be the
most wise & just, but now with new understanding.*

Day 15 - MORNING

We give thanks to you, God;
we give thanks for your name is Near,
and they tell of your wonderful deeds.

You choose and appoint the time
to be the just judge.
The earth quakes, and all its people,
and you hold her pillars firm.

I say to the arrogant, "boast not,"
and to doers of the bad, "lift not your horn;
lift not your horns against the heavens
nor speak with arrogance."

For there is no one from east or from west
and no one from the desert to exalt.
But God is the one judge,
bringing low this one and raising another.

A cup is full in the hand of Adonai,
and wine foams and mixed spice pours out.
Indeed from this they drink to her dregs,
all doers of the bad on the earth.

And I will rejoice to forever,
and sing praise to the God of Jacob.
All the horns of doers of the bad will be cut off,
and the horns of the just will be lifted up.

•

PSALM 76

Antiphon *The Son of Humanity*
is Lord also of the sabbath. Mk 2:28

God is known in Judah;
great in Israel is the Name.
In Salem is God's tent,
in Zion the dwelling place.
There flashes broke the arrow,
shield and sword, and weapons of war.

Giver of Light, you are,
more majestic than mountains of game.
Human beings of valiant heart lie plundered;
they sleep their sleep
and warriors can no more lift up their hands.
At your rebuke, God of Jacob,
both chariot and horse lie still.

You are feared, you.
Who can stand before you when you are angry?
From the heavens you pronounced judgment;
the land feared and she was quiet
when you rose, God, for the judgment
to save all the afflicted of the land.

Day 15 - MORNING

Even the angry humans come to praise you,
and you hold close the survivor of anger.
Make vows! Fulfill vows to your God Adonai!
Let all the neighbors of God bring their gift
to the One rightly feared,
who breaks the spirit of rulers,
the One rightly feared by kings and queens.

•

Son of Humanity, **ben adam**
in Hebrew, is usually translated *Son
of Man*, perhaps *Son of Human* would also
work. As Jesus applies the phrase to himself,
it is generally understood as a combination of the
vision of the glorified Just Judge at the end times in
Daniel 7, with the image of the *Servant of the Lord* (or the
Suffering Servant from four canticles of the Prophet Isaiah:
   Isaiah 42:1-4 – *A bruised reed he will not break.*
   Isaiah 49:1-7 – *I will make you a light to the nations.*
   Isaiah 50:4-11 – *I gave my back to those who beat me.*
   Isaiah 52:13-53:12 – *By his wounds we were healed.*
Folks who pray the Stations of the Cross will recognize some of this,
and so the phrase *Son of Humility* might be suggested.
Ben adam could also refer to the mystery of the incarnation,
so the phrase *Son of Woman* could also be appropriate.

PSALM 77

Antiphon   *Blessed are those who are persecuted*
for what is right, for theirs is
the reign of heaven.   Mt 5:10

I cry aloud for God, indeed I cried for help.
My cry is for God to hear me.

In the day of my distress I sought the Lord,
my hand was stretched in the night without tiring;
my soul refused to be comforted.
I remembered God and I groaned;
I meditated and my spirit grew faint.

You kept open the lids of my eyes;
I was troubled and could not speak.
I thought of former days and of years long ago.
I remembered my song in the night;
my heart mused and searched my spirit,

"Will the Lord reject to forever,
never to show favor again?
Is the unfailing love vanished to forever?
Has the promise failed for all generations?
Has God forgotten mercy
or withheld compassion in anger?"

Then I thought, "My appeal is this,
the years at the right hand of the Most High."
I will remember the deeds of Adonai;
yes, I will remember your long-ago miracles.
I will meditate on all of your works
and ponder your mighty deeds.

God in your holiness way,
what "god" is as great as God?
You are the God who does miracles;
you display among the peoples your power.
With your arm you redeemed your people,
the descendants of Jacob and Joseph.

The waters saw you, God,
the waters saw you and writhed;
indeed the depths were convulsed.
Clouds poured down waters,
thunder resounded in the skies,
and your arrows flashed around.

Your thunder sounded in the whirlwind,
lightnings lit up the world;
the earth trembled and quaked.
Through the sea is your path,
and your way through mighty waters,
though your footprints were not seen.

You led your people like the flock
by the hand of Moses and Aaron.

• • •

PSALM 78

Antiphon
*The bread of God
comes down from heaven
and gives life to the world.*   Jn 6:33

Give ear, **my people**, to my teaching.
Turn your ear to words of my mouth.
I will open my mouth in a parable;
I will utter things hidden from of old.

Our ancestors told us things we heard and know;
these we will not hide from their descendants
but tell to the next generation
the power and deeds of Adonai worthy of praise.

Statutes decreed for Jacob and laws for Israel
command our ancestors to teach their children
so the next generation will come to know;
children born will grow to tell their children.

In God will they put their trust, remembering
the deeds of El and keeping God's commands,
unlike the stubborn generation of their ancestors,
a generation of divided hearts and rebellion
and in spirit unfaithful to God.

Children of Ephraim, armed to shoot the bow,
retreated on the day of battle,
refusing to keep and live by God's covenant.

They forgot the deeds of wonder done
shown in the sight of their ancestors,
miracles in the land of Egypt, the plain of Zoan,

dividing the sea and leading them through it,
making the waters stand like a wall,
guiding them with a cloud by day
and all the night by light of fire,

splitting the rock in the desert,
giving water as abundant as the deep sea,
bringing streams from the rocky crag,
and making waters flow down like rivers.

But they kept on with the sin
rebellious in the desert against Sabaoth.
They tested God by their will
demanding the food of their craving.

Against God they questioned,
"can a table be spread in the desert by God,
whom yes we saw strike a rock
from where waters gushed and streams flowed,
and too for the people of God give meat?"

Adonai heard and was then angry
for they did not believe in God
nor trust in the deliverance.

And yet God did command the skies above
and opened doors of the heavens
and rained down for them manna to eat.

Psalm 78, continued

The humans ate the bread of angels in abundance.
And God set the east wind free from the heavens
and led by power the south wind
and rained down meat on them like dust.

Birds of flight like sand on the seashore
fell around their tents in the middle of their camp
and they ate to more than enough,
being given all of their cravings.

They did not turn from their cravings
and while their food was still in their mouths
the anger of God rose to slay their sturdy
and cut down the strong young of Israel.

Still with all this they sinned
and did not believe in the deeds of wonder done.
So their days vanished in futility
and their years in sudden death.

When God slew them they would repent
and seek and be eager for God
and remember that God is their Rock
and God Sabaoth their Redeemer.

They would flatter with their mouths
and lie to God with their tongues;
their hearts were divided
and they were unfaithful to the covenant.

But God was merciful and forgiving
and did not wipe them out,
refraining from wrath and restraining anger,
remembering that they were but flesh,
a passing breath that does not return.

How often they rebelled in the desert,
giving God grief in the wasteland.
Again and again they tested God,
vexing the Holy One of Israel.

They did not remember the power of God
nor the day of their redemption from adversity,
God's miracle signs in Egypt
and wonders in the plain of Zoan.

God turned those rivers to blood
and their streams were undrinkable.
Swarms of insects were sent and devoured,
and frogs for devastation.

Their crops were given to the grasshopper
and their produce to the locust.
With hail their vines were destroyed
and their sycamore figs with sleet.

Their cattle were given over to the hail
and their livestock to the lightning bolts.

God unleashed blazing anger against them,
wrath and indignation and hostility,
a band of angel destruction.

Psalm 78, continued

They were not spared from death
and the animals were given over to the plague.
All the firstborn of Egypt were struck,
the strong young firstfruits in the tents of Ham.

But the people of God were brought out as a flock
and led like sheep through the desert
guided in safety to be not afraid
while the sea engulfed enmity.

Thus were they brought to the holy land,
the mountain won by the right hand of God
who drove out nations from before them
and allotted from their lands an inheritance
and settled in their tents the tribes of Israel.

But they tested and rebelled against God Sabaoth
whose statutes they did not keep.
They were divided and faithless like the ancestors
and as unreliable as a bent bow.

With their high-place shrines they angered God
who was jealous because of their idols,
who heard them and became angry
and rejected Israel completely
and abandoned the shrine at Shiloh,
the very tent God set up among humans.

God gave the ark into captivity,
the glorious ark into the hands of enmity,
and the people to the sword.

Day 15 - EVENING

Their young people were consumed in fire
and heard no wedding songs;
their priests fell by the sword
and their widows could not weep.

Then the Lord woke up as from sleep
as a big strong human in a stupor from wine,
and beat back enmity to everlasting shame.

The Lord rejected the tent of Joseph
and chose not the tribe of Ephraim
but chose the tribe of Judah,
loving the Mount of Zion.

The Lord built the shrine like the heights
and like the earth established her to forever
and chose the servant David
and took him from the sheepfolds,

and brought him instead to shepherd the people,
Jacob called Israel, the heritage.
He tended them with integrity of heart
and with skillful hands he led them.

• • •

---

*Psalm 78 is
traditionally prayed in
the seasons of Lent and Easter.*

PSALM 79:1-5,9-11,13

Antiphon   *If you only knew
what makes for peace.*   Lk 19:42a

God, the nations invaded into your inheritance,
they defiled your holy temple,
they reduced Jerusalem to rubbles.
They gave the bodies of your servants
as food to birds of the air,
the flesh of your saints to beasts of earth.

They poured out their blood
like the waters around Jerusalem
and no one is left to bury.
We are a reproach to our neighbors,
scorn and derision to those around us.
Until when, Adonai, will you be angry?
Will the fire of your jealousy burn to forever?...

Help us, God of our salvation,
for the glory of your name,
and deliver us and forgive our sins
for the sake of your name.

Why should the nations say,
"Where is their God?"
Let vengeance be known among the nations
before our eyes for your servants,
for their blood being poured out.

May the groan of prisoners come before you;
and by your strong arm
preserve the condemned...

We your people, the sheep of your pasture,
will praise you to forever.
Generation to generation
will recount your praise.

•

A monk went to
Basil of Caesarea and
said, 'Speak a word, Father.'
Basil replied, 'You shall love the
Lord your God with all your heart.'
The monk went away at once. Coming
back twenty years later, the monk said, 'Abba,
I have kept the word; speak another word to me.'
Basil said, 'You shall love your neighbor as yourself.'
The monk returned in obedience to the cell to keep that also.

See *The Sayings of the Desert Fathers* by Benedicta Ward

PSALM 80

Antiphon *The reign of God will be given
to a people who produce its fruit.* Mt 21:43

Hear us, One Shepherd of Israel,
you who lead Joseph like a flock.
From your throne on the cherubim, shine forth
before Ephraim, Benjamin and Manasseh!
Awaken your might! Come to our salvation!

O God, restore us!
Make your faces shine that we may be saved!

Until when, Adonai, God of Hosts,
will you smolder against
the prayer of your people?
You fed them with bread of tears
and you made them drink tears by the bowlful.
You made us a contention to our neighbors,
and enmity mocks us.

God of Hosts, restore us!
Make your faces shine that we may be saved!

Out from Egypt, you brought a vine;
you drove out the nations and you planted it.
You cleared the ground before her;
her roots took root and she filled the land.

Day 16 - MORNING

Mountains were covered by her shade
and the mighty cedars by her branches.
She sent out her branches to the Sea,
and her shoots as far as the River.

Why have you broken down her walls?
All who pass by the way pluck her fruit.
The boar from the forest ravages her,
and creatures of the field feed on her.

God of Hosts, return now!
Look down from heaven!
See and watch over this vine,
this root that your right hand planted.
Some would burn it or cut it down;
at the rebuke of your faces may those plans perish.

Let your hand be on the one at your right hand,
the descendant of Adam you raised up for yourself.
Then we will not turn away from you;
you revive us and we will call on your name.

Adonai, God of Hosts, restore us!
Make your faces shine that we may be saved!

•

Do I qualify as an apostle, one who is sent?   (see Acts 1:21-22)
*How would I tell the great story of Jesus' baptism, ministry, death
and resurrection to a neighbor who wants to understand who I am?*

See *Forty Penances* by Stephen Joseph Wolf

PSALM 81

Antiphon *The sabbath was made for human beings,
not human beings for the sabbath.*   Mk 2:27

Sing for joy to God our strength!
Shout to the God of Jacob!

Begin the music! Strike the tambourine,
the melodious harp and the lyre!
Sound the ram horn at the new moon,
the full moon, the day of our feast!

For this is a decree for Israel,
an ordinance of the God of Jacob,
a statute established for Joseph
when time to go out from the land of Egypt.

I hear a tongue I do not know:
"I removed the burden from their shoulders,
their hands were freed from the basket.
In distress you called and I rescued you;

I answered from the thundercloud
and tested you at the waters of Meribah.
Hear, my people, and I will warn you, Israel,
if you will listen to me:

Day 16 - MORNING

'No foreign "god" shall be among you;
you shall bow to no alien "god."
I am Adonai, your God,
who brought you out of the land of Egypt.
Open wide your mouth and I will fill it!'

But my people did not listen to my voice,
and Israel did not submit to me.
So I gave them to their stubborn heart
and they followed their devices.

If my people were listening to me,
if Israel would walk in my ways,
as quickly would I subdue enmity
and turn a firm hand to adversity.

Anyone hating Adonai would cringe
under punishment lasting to forever.
But I will feed my people with finest of wheat
and satisfy you with honey out of rock."

• • •

Now says Adonai, who
created and formed you, _____;   (*pray your name*)
fear not for I have redeemed you.
I have called you by name; you are mine…
You are precious in my eyes, honored and glorious,
and I love you. I will send help and ransom for your life.
Be not afraid for I am with you.   See Isaiah 43:1-5a

PSALM 82

Antiphon
*One is the lawgiver and judge,
the one able to save and destroy;
who are you
to be judging your neighbor?*   James 4:12

God Elohim, presiding in the assembly of El,
gives judgment among little "g" gods:

"Until when will you defend the unjust
and show partiality to the faces of bad doers?
Defend the weak and the orphans!
Maintain justice for the poor and oppressed!
Rescue the weak and the needy!
Deliver them from the hands of doers of the bad!"

They know nothing and they understand nothing.
They walk in darkness
and all the foundations of earth are shaken.

"I said, 'you are gods, all of you,
sons and daughters of Elyon Most High,'
but like all humans you too will die
and like other rulers you too will fall."

Rise up, Elohim, and judge the earth!
For to you belong all the nations!

•   Note: Psalm 83 is omitted in the *Litrugy of the Hours*.

Day 16 - EVENING

PSALM 84

Antiphon *Why do you look for me?*
Do you not know that I have to be
in my Abba's house?   Lk 2:49

How lovely are your dwellings,
Adonai Sabaoth!
My soul she yearns and even faints
for the courts of Adonai;
my heart and my flesh cry out for God alive.

Even the sparrow found a home
and the swallow a nest for her
where she may settle her young ones
near your altar, Adonai Sabaoth,
my Ruler and my God.

Blessed are the dwellers in your house,
ever they praise you.
Blessed are the ones whose strength is in you,
who make a pilgrimage in their hearts.

Passing through the Baca Valley,
springs are found,
pools covered over with autumn rains.
They go from strength to strength
and appear before God in Zion.

Psalm 84, continued

Adonai, God Sabaoth, hear my prayer!
Listen, God of Jacob. God, our shield, look!
Look on the face of your anointed one!

Better is one day in your courts
than a thousand elsewhere.
Better to be doorkeeper in my God's house
than to dwell in tents of those who do the bad,

for God Adonai is sun and shield.
Adonai bestows grace and honor,
withholding no goodness
from blameless walkers.

Adonai Sabaoth,
blessed is the one trusting in you.

•

*Psalm 84
is often used
for the blessing
of a new sacred space.*

Day 16 - EVENING

PSALM 85

Antiphon   *Take courage;*
            it is me. Come.   Mt 14:27,29

You showed favor, Adonai, to your land;
you restored the fortune of Jacob.
You forgave the iniquity of your people;
you pardoned all of their sin.
You set aside all of your wrath;
you turned from your fierce anger.

Restore us, God of our salvation!
And put away your displeasure toward us.
Will you be angry with us to forever?
Will you prolong your anger
to generation and generation?

Will you not revive us again
that your people may rejoice in you?
Show us, Adonai, your unfailing love
and grant us your salvation.

I will listen to what El Adonai will say,
promising peace to the people, even to the saints,
but not letting them return to folly.
Surely near to those in awe is their salvation,
the glory to dwell in our land.

Psalm 85, continued

Love and Fidelity meet;
Justice and Peace kiss.
Fidelity springs forth from the earth
and Justice looks down from the heavens.

Indeed Adonai will give the good
and our land will yield her harvest,
Justice going forward to prepare the way
for the steps of the Lord.

• • •

Day 17 - MORNING

PSALM 86

Antiphon *Leave both the weed and the wheat*
to grow together until the harvest. Mt 13:30

Hear in your ear, Adonai;
answer me for I am poor and needy.
Guard my life for I am devoted;
save your servant, my God,
the one trusting in you.

Have mercy on me, Lord,
for to you I call all the day.
Bring joy to your servant,
for to you, Lord, I lift up my soul.

Indeed, Lord, you are kind and forgiving
and abundant in love for all who call to you.
Hear my prayer, Adonai;
listen to the sound of my cries for mercy.

In the day of my trouble I will call to you
for you will answer me.
There is none like you among so-called "gods"
and there are no deeds like yours, Lord.

All the nations you made will come
and they will worship before you, Lord,
and they will bring glory to your name
for you are great and do marvelous deeds,
you, God, you yourself.

Psalm 86, continued

Teach me, Adonai, your way
and I will walk in your truth.
Undivide my heart
that I may fear your name.

I will praise you, Lord my God, with all my heart
and I will glorify your name to forever
for great is your love of me
and you deliver my soul from the depth of Sheol.

Arrogant ones attack against me, God;
a band of ruthless people seek my life
and do not regard you before them.

But you, Lord El, Compassionate and Gracious,
are slow of anger and abundant in love and fidelity.
Turn to me! And have mercy on me!

Grant your strength to your servant
and save the child of your handservant!
Give to me a sign of goodness
that enmity may see and find shame,
for you, Adonai, help me and comfort me.

•

To praise you, Lord, is the desire
of the human, a little piece of your creation.
You stir us to take pleasure in praising you, for you have
made us for yourself, and our heart is restless until it rests in you.
from *Confessions* by Saint Augustine of Hippo

PSALM 87

Antiphon　　　*The Abba and I are one.*　　　Jn 10:30

On the holy mountain
is the foundation of Adonai,
who loves the gates of Zion
more than all of Jacob's dwellings.
Glorious things are being said of you, city of God.

"I will record Rahab and Babylon
among those who know me;
see Philistia and Tyre with Ethiopia:
this one was born there!"

But of Zion it will be said,
"One and another were born in her,
and the Most High will establish her."

Adonai will write when registering peoples,
"This one was born there."
And making music they will sing,
"All of my fountains are in you."

•

In the Bible
a mountain is often
a meeting place with God.

PSALM 88

Antiphon *Leave the dead to bury their own dead;
   you go proclaim the reign of God.* Lk 9:60

Adonai, **Elohay**, my Savior,
I cry out day and night before you.
May my prayer come before you;
turn your ear to my cry.

My soul is full of troubles
and my life draws near to Sheol.
I am counted among those
going down to the pit,
like a human with no strength,

set apart with the dead ones
like slain ones lying in the grave,
whom you no longer remember,
whom are cut off from your care.

You put me in the pit of the lowest,
in the darkest deep.
Your anger lies heavy upon me
and all your waves overwhelm.

Day 17 - MORNING

You took friends away from me
and made me repulsive to them;
in confinement I cannot escape.
My eye is dim from grief;
I call to you, Adonai,
and in every day spread my hands to you.

Is it to the dead ones you show wonder?
Do the dead rise up and praise you?
Is your love declared in the grave
or your fidelity in the no-more?
Is your wonder known in the darkness
or your righteous deeds in the land of oblivion?

But to you, Adonai, I cry for help;
in the morning my prayer comes before you.
Why do you reject my self, Adonai?
Why hide your faces from me?

Afflicted and coming close to death
and despairing from youth,
I have suffered your terrors.
Your anger has swept over me
and your terrors destroy me.

They surround me all the day like the floods,
engulfing over me completely.
You took far away my loving companion;
my one friend is darkness.

• • •

PSALM 89:2-38

Antiphon
*One loving father or mother
or son or daughter
more than me
is not worthy of me.*   Mt 10:37

Forever will I sing the great love of Adonai;
with my mouth I will make known
your fidelity to generation and generation.
Indeed I will declare forever love standing firm,
your faithfulness established in the heavens.

"I made a covenant with my chosen ones,
sworn to my servant David.
I will establish your line to forever,
and to generation and generation
I will make firm your throne."

The heavens praise your wonder, Adonai,
and your fidelity in the holy assembly.
For who in the sky can compare to Adonai;
who is like Adonai among heavenly beings?

God is greatly feared in the council of holy ones
and is awesome over all who surround around.
Adonai Sabaoth, who is like you?
Mighty Adonai, your fidelity is around you.

You rule over the surging of the sea;
when waves mount up you still them.
You crushed Rahab like the slain
and scattered enmity
with the arm of your strength.

To you are the heavens and to you is the earth;
the world and all her fullness you founded.
North and South you created;
Tabor and Hermon sing for joy at your name.

To you is the arm strong with power;
your hand is exalted, your right hand.
Justice and Judgment
are the foundation of your throne;
Hesed-Love and Fidelity go before your faces.

Blessed are people who learn to acclaim Adonai;
they walk in the light of your presences.
In your name they rejoice all the day
and in your judgment they exult,

for you are the glory of their strength
and by your favor you exalt our horn.
Indeed Adonai is our shield
and the Holy One of Israel is our Ruler.

Once in a vision you spoke to your faithful ones:
"I bestowed strength on a warrior;
I raised from the people a young man.

Psalm 89, continued

I chose David my servant,
I anointed him with my sacred oil,
and my hand will sustain him;
surely my arm will strengthen him.

Enmity will not subject him to tribute
and people doing the bad will not oppress him.
Before him I will crush foes
and strike down adversity,

and my fidelity and my love are with him,
and through my hands will his horn be exalted.
And I will set his hand over the sea
and his right hand over the rivers.

He will call out to me: 'You are my Father,
my God and Rock of my salvation.'
I will also appoint him firstborn
and most exalted among rulers of the earth.

I will maintain my love for him to forever
and my unfailing covenant with him.
I will establish his line to forever
and his throne as days of the heavens.

If his sons and daughters forsake my law
and do not follow my statutes,
if they violate my decrees
and keep not my commands,

Day 17 - EVENING

then I will punish their sins with the rod
and their iniquity with floggings.
But I will not take my love from them,
nor will I ever betray my fidelity.

I will not violate my covenant
nor will I alter the utterance of my lips.
Once I swore by my holiness;
I will not lie to David:

His line will continue to forever
and his throne like the sun before me.
Like the moon it is established forever,
a faithful witness in the sky."

•

Hounded by somebody about something,
a brother said, 'You are on it, but here is my list:
God, family, job, parish, etc... I want to keep you on it,
but you will not be first on my list. Can I keep you on my list?'

PSALM 89:39-53

Antiphon *Who does not take their cross*
and follow after me
is not worthy of me.   Mt 10:38

Lord, you have rejected and spurned,
you were angry with your anointed one.
You renounced the covenant of your servant,
the crown you defiled in the dust.

You broke through all of the walls
and reduced the strongholds to ruin.
Those passing on the way plundered
and the neighbors were full of scorn.

You exalted the right hand of adversity
and made enmity rejoice.
You turned back the edge of our sword
and did not support us in the battle.

You put an end to the splendor
and cast the throne to the ground.
You cut short the days of youth
and covered us over with shame.

Until when, Adonai?
Will you hide yourself to forever?
Will your wrath burn like fire?
Remember how fleeting am I!

Day 17 - EVENING

For what futility you created the human race,
sons and daughters of Adam and Eve!
What human can live and not see death,
or save the self from the power of Sheol?

Where, Lord, are your former great loves,
your fidelity sworn to David?
Remember, Lord,
the mockery of your servants!

I bear this in my heart
from many nations, Adonai:
the mockery of enmity,
the mockery of the steps of your anointed one.

Blessed be Adonai to forever.
Amen and amen.

• • •

My Cross:

Part of the faith journey
is to figure out what my cross is.
Hint: everyone carries a core wound.
Then I can run away from it, try to give
it to someone else, pretend to know nothing
about it, try to bury it, or take it up and follow Jesus.

PSALM 90

Antiphon *Be wary and on guard against all greed
for life is not about possessions.* Lk 12:15

You, Lord, you have been our refuge
from generation to generation.
Before the mountains were born,
before you brought forth earth,
from eternity to eternity, you are God.

You turn humans back to dust and say,
"Return, sons and daughters of humanity."
A thousand years in your eyes
are like the day yesterday that went by,
like one watch of the night.

You sweep humans into the sleep
like new grass in the morning that sprouts:
in the morning it springs up and sprouts
and then by the evening is withered and dry.

Indeed we can be consumed in your anger
and terrified by your indignation.
You set our iniquities before you,
our secrets in the light of your presences.

Indeed all our days pass away under your anger;
we finish our years like a sigh.
Our days last for seventy years
or eighty if given the strength.

Day 18 - MORNING

The best part of them are trouble and sorrow,
passing quickly, and we fly away.
Who knows the power of your anger,
who fears your wrath?

Number our days aright;
teach, that we may gain hearts of wisdom.
How long, Adonai, until you relent?
Have compassion on your servants.

Satisfy our morning hunger
with your unfailing love
that we may sing for joy and be glad all our days.
Make us glad, equal to our affliction,
the years of trouble we have seen.

May your deeds be shown to your servants
and your splendor to their children.
May the favor of the Lord our God rest upon us
and the work of our hands be made good;
yes, make good the work of our hands.

•

Psalm 90
is used in the ritual for
blessing of a place of business.

See also the prayer for Workers on page 95.

PSALM 91

Antiphon
*It has been written,
"not on bread alone
shall the human live."*   Lk 4:4

One who dwells in the shelter of Elyon,
in the shadow of Shaddai, will find rest.
I will say of Adonai, my refuge, my fortress:
in my God do I trust.

Surely the Lord will save you
from fowler snare, from deadly pestilence.
With the feather of the Lord you will be covered,
and under those wings you will find refuge,
shield and rampart, the fidelity of the Lord.

You will have no fear of terror at night
nor of arrows flying by day,
of pestilence stalking in the darkness,
nor of plague that destroys at midday.

A thousand may fall at your side,
and ten thousand at your right hand;
near to you they will not come.

Observe with your eyes, simply watch;
punishment of doers of the bad you will see.
Make Adonai, who is my refuge,
make Elyon your dwelling.

Harm will not befall you,
nor will disaster come near your tent.
God's own Angels, the Lord will command
to guard you in all of your ways.

In their hands they will lift you up;
your foot will not strike against the stone.
Upon lion and cobra you will tread,
you will trample the great lion and serpent.

"Because you love me, I will rescue you,
I will protect all who know my Name.
You will call upon me and I will answer.
I am with you in trouble;
I will deliver you and honor you.

In length of days I will satisfy you,
and show you my salvation."

•

Psalm 91 is often used for night prayer
with the Canticle of Simeon (Luke 2:29-32 on page 30)
and the antiphon:

Protect us Lord as we stay awake, watch over us as we sleep
that awake we may keep watch with Christ
and asleep rest in his peace.

or *Lord, save/ us! Save/ us while \ we are a-wake \,*
pro-tect us while we are a-sleep, that we may keep our watch/
with Christ/, and when we sleep \, rest/ in his \ peace.

PSALM 92:1-9,11,13-16

Antiphon *The reign of God is as when*
a human might throw seed on the earth
and sleep and rise night and day
and the seed sprouts and grows
without the human knowing how.   Mk 4:26,27

It is good to praise Adonai,
to make music to your name, Most High,
to proclaim your love in the morning
and your fidelity at night
on the ten-string and on the lyre,
and the melody of the harp.

For you make me glad by your deeds, Adonai;
at the works of your hands I sing for joy.
How great are your works, Adonai;
very profound are your thoughts.
The senseless human does not know
and the fool does not understand.

Though the bad can spring up like grass
and doers of the bad seem to flourish,
their ways will be destroyed to forever.
But you, Adonai, are on high to forever…

Day 18 - MORNING

You gave me strength like a wild ox
and I was anointed with fresh oil…
The just will flourish like the palm tree,
and grow like a cedar of Lebanon.

Planted in the house of Adonai,
in the courts of our God they will flourish.
In old age they will still bear fruit,
ever full of sap and still green,
to proclaim, "Adonai is just,
in my Rock there is no wrong."

• • •

---

*Though the
psalms originated
very many centuries ago
in the East, they express accurately
the pain and hope, the unhappiness and trust,
of people of every age and country, and celebrate
especially faith in God, revelation and redemption…
The person who prays the psalms in the name of the
church can always find a reason for joy or sadness.*
See *Introduction to the Liturgy of the Hours,* 107

*Come Holy Spirit,
take hold of my life, and
sign me with your holy love;
give me your gifts, confirm me in faith.
Spirit come.*

Serafina Di Giacomo

Day 18 - EVENING

PSALM 93

Antiphon   *Do you ask if I am a ruler from yourself
or have others told you about me?*   Jn 18:34

Adonai reigns, robed in majesty;
robed is Adonai and armed with strength.

The world is firmly established;
she cannot be moved.
Your throne was set up from long ago;
from eternity you are.

The seas lifted up, Adonai,
the seas lifted up their voice;
the seas lifted up their pounding.

More than thunders of great waters
or mighty breakers of the sea,
mighty in the height is Adonai.

Your statutes stand very firm;
your house, Adonai, is adorned in holiness
for length of days.

•

---

*O God,
your sea is so great
and my boat is so small.*
Breton fishing prayer

PSALM 94

Antiphon *Jesus touched her hand, the fever left her,
and rising she began serving them.* Mt 8:15

God of vindication,
Adonai, God of vindication, shine forth!
Rise up, One Judge of the earth!
Pay back desserts to the proud!

Until when, Adonai, will doers of the bad?
Until when will doers of the bad be jubilant?
They pour out and speak arrogance;
all the doers of the bad make boast.

They crush your people, Adonai,
and they oppress your very own.
They slay the widow and alien;
they murder the orphan.

They say Adonai does not see
and the God of Jacob pays no heed.
Take heed, senseless ones among the people;
fools, when will you become wise?

Does the one who shapes the ear not hear?
Does the one who forms the eye not see?
Will the one who disciplines nations not punish?
Will the one who teaches have no knowledge?

Adonai knows the thoughts of humans,
that they are puffs of air.

Blessed is the one you instruct, Adonai,
the one you teach from your law
to grant relief from days of trouble
till a pit is dug for doers of the bad,

for the people of Adonai will not be rejected,
your very own never forsaken.
Judgment will again be just;
all the upright of heart will follow it.

Who will rise up for me against doers of the bad?
Who will take a stand against people doing bad?
Unless Adonai helps me,
I would as soon dwell in the silence of my self.

When I said, "My foot slips,"
your love, Adonai, supported me.
When my anxieties were great inside me
your consolations brought joy to my soul.

Can a throne of corruptions be allied with you,
one that brings misery by decree?
They band together against the life of the just
and condemn the innocent to death.

But Adonai became to me as a fortress,
and my God as a rock of refuge.
A rock of refuge is my God,
who will repay their sin to them
and destroy their bad ways.
Our God, Adonai, will destroy them.

• • •

PSALM 95

Antiphon   *Where two or three*
           are gathered in my name,
           there am I in the midst of them.   Mt 18:20

Come, let us sing to Adonai;
let us shout to our saving Rock.
Let us come before the faces with gratitude
and make a joyful noise with song.

Adonai is the great El,
the great Ruler above all those little "g" gods,
holding in hand the depths of earth
and peaks of mountains,
the sea and dry land formed by the hand.

Come, let us worship and bow and kneel
before Adonai who made us.
For God is our God, and we are the people
of the pasture and flock and care of our God.

"If today you hear this voice
do not harden your heart,
as at Meribah and the desert day at Massah
where your ancestors tested me;
they tried me though they saw my work.

For forty years was my anger on that generation,
the people straying in their heart;
and so they did not know my ways,
and so were unable to enter my rest."

•

---

*The world is making a discovery that there
is and always has been a regularly occurring
non-pathological minority variant in the human
condition known in our time as being lesbian, gay,
bi-sexual, transgender, queer, intersex, asexual, +.
So what will we do with this discovery?*

See writings of James Alison, Theologian

PSALM 96

Antiphon *Render to Ceasar the things of Ceasar,*
and to God the things of God. Mt 22:21

Sing to Adonai a new song!
Sing to Adonai, all the earth!
Sing to Adonai and praise the name!
Proclaim salvation from day to day!

Declare among the nations the glory of the Lord!
Among all the peoples the marvelous deeds,
for great is Adonai, greatly being praised,
the one to be feared above all so-called "gods."

For all "gods" of the nations
are do-nothing idols,
but Adonai made the heavens,
splendor and majesty and strength and glory
in the holy sanctuary.

Ascribe to Adonai, families of nations!
Acknowledge Adonai as glory and strength!
Give to Adonai the glory of the Name!

Bring offerings and come into the courts!
Worship Adonai in holy splendor!
Tremble in the presence all you earth!

Say among the nations, "Adonai is our ruler!"
Firmly set, the world cannot be moved
and peoples will be judged with equity.

Let the heavens rejoice and the earth be glad.
Let the sea resound and all its fullness.
Let the fields and all that is in them be jubilant
and all the trees of the forests sing for joy

before Adonai who comes,
who comes to judge the earth,
who will judge the world and its peoples
with justice and honesty.

●

Praying the
psalms continually
ponders and proclaims
the action of God in the history
of salvation.   Pope Paul VI, 1970

PSALM 97

Antiphon *Fill the water pots with water;*
now draw and carry some
to the master of the feast.   Jn 2:7,8

Adonai reigns; let the earth be glad.
Let all the distant shores rejoice.
Clouds and thick darkness surround the throne
founded on justice and right.

Fire goes before,
consuming enmity on every side.
Lightnings light up the world;
the earth sees and trembles.

Mountains melt like wax before Adonai,
before the Lord of all the earth.
The heavens proclaim God's justice
and all peoples see the glory.

Let those who worship idols be shamed,
those boasting in their images.
Worship God, all you "gods."

Zion hears and rejoices
and the villages of Judah are glad
because of your judgments, Adonai.

Day 19 - MORNING

For you, Adonai,
are Most High over all the earth,
far exalted above all the "gods."

The bad is despised by lovers of Adonai,
who guards the lives of faithful ones
and delivers them from the hands
of doers of the bad.

Light dawns for the just
and joy for the honest of heart.
Rejoice in Adonai, you just,
and praise the holy name.

• • •

Contemplation is the realization of
God in our life, not just realization
of an idea or something partial, but
a realization of the whole thing – the
realization that we belong totally to God
and God has given Godself totally to us.
It has all happened and it is going on now…
You don't really see this. It happens and you
see it and you don't. You get glimpses of it, you
believe it, your life is based on it, and sometimes it
seems to be in complete contradiction or impossible, and
yet it is there. It is the place we are always coming back to.
See *Why We Live In Community* by Thomas Merton

PSALM 98

Antiphon *I will give you a mouth and wisdom that will not be contradicted or withstood.* Lk 21:15

Sing to Adonai a new song
who has done marvelous things,
working salvation at the right hand and holy arm.

Adonai made known salvation,
justice revealed for the eyes of the nations.
Love is remembered
and fidelity to the house of Israel

and all the ends of the earth see
the salvation of our God.
Shout for joy to Adonai, all you earth!
Break into song and sing praise.

Make music to Adonai with harp,
with harp and the sound of singing,
with trumpets and blast of ram horn:
Shout for joy before Adonai, the Ruler.

Let the sea resound, the fullness of the world,
and those living in her.
Let the rivers clap hands,
let the mountains sing together for joy

before Adonai who comes to judge the earth,
who will judge the world with justice
and peoples with equity.

●

PSALM 99

Antiphon	*Were not ten lepers cleansed?*	
	And this one foreigner alone	
	gives glory to God?	Lk 17:17

Adonai reigns; let the nations tremble.
The One sits enthroned on the cherubim;
let the earth shake.

Great in Zion is Adonai,
and exalted over all of the nations.
Let them praise your great and awesome name,
"Holy are you, and mighty."

The Ruler of justice loves you
and establishes equity and justice,
having done what is right in Jacob.

Exalt Adonai, our God!
And worship at the feet on the footstool,
"Holy are you, and mighty."

Moses and Aaron were among the priests,
and Samuel among those calling the name,
calling on El Adonai, who answered them,
who spoke to them from the pillar of cloud.
They kept the statutes and decrees given to them.

Psalm 99, continued

Adonai, our God, you answered them.
You were the one Forgiving El to them,
though punishing their misdeeds.

Exalt Adonai our God!
And worship at the holy mountain,
for holy is our God Adonai!

•

Day 19 - EVENING

PSALM 100

Antiphon   *Go to the lost sheep*
           of the house of Israel.   Mt 10:6

Shout for joy to Adonai, all you earth!
Serve Adonai with gladness!
Come into the presence with joyful song.

Know that Adonai is God, who made us,
whose people we are,
in whose pasture we are the sheep.

Enter the gates with thanksgiving,
go into the courts with praise!
Give thanks and give praise to the Name!

Good is Adonai, and loving to forever,
and faithful through generations and generation.

•

Lord, do for me today what I cannot do for myself.
See *The Anonymous Disciple* by Gerard Goggins

PSALM 101

Antiphon *A great prophet is risen among us,*
and God has visited the people of God. Lk 7:16

I will sing of *hesed* love and justice;
to you, Adonai, I will sing praise.
I will take care to act with integrity in life.
When will you come to me?

I will walk with integrity of heart
in the midst of my house.
I hate and will not set before my eyes
vile things that faithless people do;
they will not cling to me.

The corrupt heart will be far from me;
I will know nothing of the bad.
I will silence the secret slandering of a neighbor;
haughty eyes and proud hearts I will not endure.

My eyes are on the faithful of the land,
to dwell with me;
one who walks in a way of integrity
can be in my service.

Anyone practicing deceit
will not dwell in the midst of my house;
nor will one speaking falsehoods
stand before my eyes.

Each morning I will silence bad doers in the land
to cut off doings of bad things
from the city of Adonai.

• • •

PSALM 102

Antiphon   *Whoever is not against you*
             is for you.   Lk 9:50

Adonai, hear my prayer
and let my cry for help come to you.
Hide not your faces from me
on the day of my distress.
Turn your ear to me on the day I call!
Quickly! Answer me!

My days vanish like smoke
and my bones burn like a glowing ember.
My heart is blighted like the grass
and so withered that I forget to eat my food.
Because of my loud groaning
my bones cling to my skin.

I am like a desert owl;
like an owl of the ruins lying awake,
I became like a bird alone on the housetop.
Enmity taunts me all the day,
railing against me, cursing by me.

I eat ash as food and mingle my drink with tears
because of your anger and your wrath,
for you took me up and threw me aside.
My days are like the long shadow,
and like the grass I wither away.

But you, Adonai, sit enthroned to forever;
your renown is to generation and generation.
You will arise.
You will have compassion on Zion,
for the time to show favor to her,
the appointed time, has come,
for her stones are dear to your servants
and her dust moves them to pity.

The nations will fear your name, Adonai,
and all the rulers of the earth your glory.
Adonai will rebuild Zion and appear in glory
and respond to the prayers of the destitute
and not despise their plea.

Let this be written for future generations
that people yet to be created may praise Yah.
Adonai looked down
from the high sanctuary place
viewing from heavens to earth,
to hear the groans of prisoners
and release those doomed to death

Declare in Zion the name of Adonai
and give praise in Jerusalem
when peoples assemble together,
and nations, to give worship.

Psalm 102, continued

Adonai broke my strength in mid-course
and cut short my days, and I said, "My El,
take me not away in the midst of my days.
Your years are through generation of generations.

In the beginning you founded the earth
and the heavens, the work of your hands.
They will perish, but you remain;
they will all wear out like a garment;
like clothing you will change them
and they will be discarded.

But you: the same; your years will never end.
Children of your servants will live
and their descendants
will be established before you."

•

*Let us not look back
to the past with anger
nor to the future with fear
but around with awareness.*

James Thurber, cartoonist d. 1961

Day 20 - MORNING

PSALM 103

Antiphon   *Forgive each of your siblings*
            from your heart.   Mt 18:35

My soul, praise Adonai!
All my inmost being, praise the holy Name!
My soul, praise Adonai,
whose benefits are not to be forgotten:

forgiveness of all your sins,
healing of all your diseases,
redemption of your life from the pit,
crowning you with love and compassion,
satisfying your desire with good,
renewing your youths like the eagle,
working vindication
and justice for all who are oppressed.

Adonai's ways are made known to Moses
and the deeds to peoples of Israel.

Compassionate and gracious is Adonai,
slow to anger and abundant in love,
neither accusing to always
nor harboring anger to forever,
neither treating us in accord with our sins
nor repaying us in accord with our iniquities.

Psalm 103, continued

As high as the heavens are above the earth
so great is the love for ones who fear Adonai.
As far as the east is from the west
so far from us are our transgressions removed.

As a parent has compassion on a child,
so has Adonai compassion on those in awe,
knowing our form and remembering we are dust.

The days of a human are like the grass
flourishing like flowers of the field,
for wind blows over and it is no more
and the place remembers it no more.

But the love of Adonai for the awestruck
is from everlasting to everlasting,
with favor for children of their children,
of those keeping the covenant
and remembering to obey the precepts.

Adonai established a throne in the heavens,
a reign to rule over all.
Praise Adonai, you angels,
you strong and mighty ones doing the bidding,
obeying the voice of the word.

Praise Adonai, you hosts,
you serving and doing the will.
Praise Adonai, all you works,
in all places of the dominion.
My soul, praise Adonai!

• • •

Day 20 - EVENING

PSALM 104

Antiphon   *Peace to you;*
as the Abba has sent me, so I send you;
receive the Holy Spirit.   Jn 20:21

Soul of me, praise Adonai!
My God, Adonai, you are beyond measure.
Splendor and majesty clothe you,
wrapped in light as a garment,

stretching out over the heavens like a tent,
laying beams on the waters of the upper chambers.
You make a chariot of the clouds,
riding on wings of wind,
making messengers of the winds
and servants of flaming fire.

You have set foundations on earth,
unmoveable for ever and ever.
Deep is your garment, covering the earth;
above the mountains the waters stood.

At your rebuke, they then fled;
at the sound of your thunder they took flight.
They flowed over mountains
and went down into valleys
to the places you assigned for them.
You set a boundary they are not to cross;
never again are they to cover the earth.

Psalm 104, continued

You make springs of water pour into ravines;
between the mountains they flow.
They give drink to all beasts of the field;
they quench the thirst of donkeys.
Birds of the air nest in branches beside them;
they give you their song.

You water mountains from your upper chambers;
by the fruit of your works the earth is satisfied.
You make grass grow for the cattle
and plants for human beings to cultivate

to bring forth food from the earth,
wine to make glad the human heart,
oil to make faces shine,
and bread to sustain the human heart.

They are all Adonai's well watered trees,
cedars of Lebanon planted
where birds make their nests,
and the pine tree where the stork makes a home,
mountains, the high ones, for wild goats,
and crags, a refuge for rock badgers.

You made the moon to mark off seasons
and the sun that knows when to set.
You bring darkness
and all beasts of the forest prowl in the night.
The lions roar for prey
seeking their food from God.

Day 20 - EVENING

The sun rises, they steal away,
and into their dens they lie down.
Human beings go out to do their work
and labor until the evening.

How varied are your works, Adonai!
All of them in wisdom you made.
The earth is full of your creatures.

There is the sea, vast and spacious;
living creatures countless there,
small ones and large ones.
There ships go about
and leviathan which you formed for frolic.

All of them look to you
to give them food at their time.
You give to them and they gather,
you open your hands
and they are goodly satisfied.

You hide your face and they are lost,
you take away their breath and they die
and to their dust they return.
You breathe your Spirit, and they are created,
and you renew the faces of earth.

May the glory of Adonai endure to forever.
May Adonai rejoice in these works:
looking at the earth, she trembles,
touching the mountains, they smoke.

Psalm 104, continued

I will sing to Adonai during my life
and sing praise to my God while I still am.
May my meditation be found pleasing.
I rejoice in Adonai.
May sin vanish from the earth
and the bad be done no more.

Praise Adonai, my soul!
Hallelujah!

• • •

Hallelujah!
It means, "Praise God"!
Can you now and then raise your
hands in the air and say, even quietly,
"God, I praise you"? It's OK that some of us
must go to our inner room and close the door to do this.

When you pray, enter your room and close your door
and pray to your Abba in secret.   Mt 6:6

Day 21 - MORNING

PSALM 105

Antiphon *Simeon sang in the temple
of seeing salvation,
a light for revelation to the nations.* Lk 2:29-32

Give thanks to Adonai; call on the Name.
Make known among the nations the Lord's deeds!

Glory be to the holy Name;
let the heart of the seeker of Adonai rejoice.
Look to Adonai, to the strength;
seek always the faces of the Lord.

Remember the deeds of wonder done,
the miracles and the judgments mouthed,
you descendants and servants of Abraham,
you chosen ones of Jacob.

Adonai is our God, judge in all the earth,
remembering the covenant to forever
commanded for a thousand generations,
the word made with Abraham,
the oath to Isaac,

confirmed to Jacob as a decree,
to Israel as an everlasting covenant:
"I will give to you land of Canaan,
a portion of your inheritance."

Psalm 105, continued

When they were few, few in numbers,
with strangers in their midst,
then they wandered from nation to nation,
from one people to another.

No one was allowed to oppress them
and for their sake rulers were rebuked:
"Do not touch my anointed ones;
do no harm to my prophets."

Famine was allowed onto the land
and the ruler's food supply was destroyed.
A man Joseph was sent before them,
sold as a slave;
they bruised his foot with the shackle

and his neck entered the irons
till the time foretold of him came to pass.
The word of Adonai proved him true.
The ruler sent for him and released him;

the ruler of the peoples set him free
and made him master of his household
and ruler over all his possessions
to instruct the royals as was his pleasure
and to teach the elders.

Then Israel entered Egypt;
Jacob lived as an alien in the land of Ham.

This people became very numerous,
more fruitful than their others.
The hearts of the rulers were turned to hate
and conspired against this servant people.

Moses was sent as servant of the Lord
and Aaron as chosen of the Lord.
They performed the deeds of the Lord,
signs and wonders in the land of Ham.

The Lord sent darkness and it was dark;
for they rebelled against the word.
Their waters were turned into blood
which caused their fish to die.

Their land was teemed with frogs,
even the bedrooms of their rulers.
Swarms of flies were sent at a word,
gnats through all of their country.

Their rains were turned into hail
and lightning flamed through their land.
Their vine and fig tree were struck down
and the trees of their country were shattered.

Locusts came at the word
and grasshoppers without number.
Every green thing in their land was eaten up,
eaten up with the produce of their soil.

Psalm 105, continued

Then their firstborn were struck down, all of them,
the firstfruit of their humanity in all of their land.

The Lord brought them out with silver and gold
and no one faltered among the tribes.
Egypt was glad when they left, glad with dread.

A cloud as a cover was spread out
and fire to give them light at night.
They asked for quail and the Lord brought it
and satisfied them with bread from heaven.

The rock was opened and waters gushed out
flowing in the desert as a river,
for the holy promise was remembered,
the promise made to servant Abraham,
and the people were brought out rejoicing,
the chosen ones with shouts of joy.

They received the lands of nations
and inherited the toil of peoples
so that they might keep the precepts
and observe the laws of the Lord.

Hallelujah!

• • •

Day 21 - EVENING

PSALM 106:1-16,19-48

Antiphon *Whose sins you forgive, they are forgiven;*
whose sins you hold, they are held.   Jn 20:23

Hallelujah!
Give thanks to Adonai who is good,
whose love is to forever.

Who can proclaim the mighty acts of Adonai?
Who can tell the fullness of praise?
Blessed are they who maintain justice,
doing just deeds at all times.

Remember me, Adonai, as you favor your people!
In your salvation, come with your aid for me
to enjoy the prosperity of your chosen ones,
to have joy in the joy of your nation,
and to give praise with your inheritance.

We have sinned as did our ancestors;
we have done wrong with bad deeds.
Our ancestors when in Egypt
gave no thought to your miracle deeds,
did not remember your many kindnesses,
and rebelled by *Yam Suf*, the Sea of Reeds.

Still you saved them for the sake of your name,
to make known your power.
You rebuked the Sea of Reeds; it dried up.
You led them through the depths as the desert.

Psalm 106, continued

And you saved them from the hands of hostility
and redeemed them from the power of enmity.

The waters covered the adversity;
not one of them survived.
Then they believed in the promises made,
and sang out praise.

But soon did they forget those deeds
and would not wait for good counsel.
They craved cravings in the desert
and in the wasteland they tested their El,
who gave them their request
but sent a wasting disease on their life.

They envied Moses in the camp
and Aaron, the consecrated of Adonai…
They made a calf at Horeb
and gave their worship to a cast idol.
They exchanged their Glory
for an image of a grass-eating bull.

They forgot El who had saved them,
doing great things in Egypt,
miracle deeds in the land of Ham
and awesome deeds by the Sea of Reeds.

By a word spoken they were to be destroyed,
except that Moses the chosen stood in the breach.
Then they despised the beautiful land
and did not believe the promise made.

They grumbled in their tents
and did not obey the voice of Adonai,
who lifted a hand to let them fall in the desert
and their descendants fall among the nations;
they were scattered through the lands.

They yoked themselves to Baal of Peor
and they ate of sacrifices to lifeless ones.
They provoked anger by their deeds
and a plague broke out among them.

Phinehas stood up and intervened
and the plague was checked;
this was credited to him as a just and good deed
for generation and generations to forever.

They angered by the waters of Meribah,
the cause of trouble for Moses,
who spoke rashly with his lips
when they made his spirit bitter.

They did not defeat the peoples as commanded,
but mingled with the nations
and adopted their customs.
They worshiped their idols
which became to them as a snare.

Psalm 106, continued

They sacrificed their sons and daughters.
They shed the innocent blood
of their own sons and daughters
whom they sacrificed to idols of Canaan,
desecrating the land by this blood.

They defiled themselves by their deeds
and prostituted themselves in their doings.
Against the people grew the anger of Adonai,
abhorring the promised inheritance.

Into the hands of nations they were given,
ruled by adversity, oppressed by enmity,
and made subject to their power.
Many times were they delivered,
but they rebelled in their decisions
and wasted away in their guilt.

And yet on hearing their cry
the Lord took note of their distress
and remembered for them the covenant
and relented in abundant love
bringing to them compassion
from even their captors.

Save us, Adonai our God!
Gather us from the nations
to give thanks to your holy name
and glory in your praise.

Day 21 - EVENING

Blessed be Adonai, God of Israel
from everlasting to everlasting
and let all the people say, "Amen!"
Hallelujah!

• • •

Bless us, O Lord, with discontent
at easy answers, half-truths, and superficiality,
that we may live out of the depths of our hearts.
Bless us, O Lord, with anger
at injustice, oppression, and exploitation of people,
that we may work for justice, freedom and peace.
Bless us, O Lord, with tears to shed
for those who suffer from pain, rejection, starvation, and war,
that we may reach out hands of Christ that bring comfort.
And bless us, O Lord, with enough foolishness
to believe that your way makes all the difference
so that your desire may be fulfilled.

adapted from a blessing by Sr. Ruth Fox, OSB

PSALM 107

Antiphon *In awe, the disciples asked,
who then is this, whom
both the wind and the sea obey?*   Mk 4:41

"**Give thanks** to Adonai, who is good,
whose love is to forever."

Let this be said by the redeemed of Adonai,
who redeemed them from the hand of enmity
and gathered them from the lands,
from east and west, from north and the south sea.

Some wandered in the desert wasteland,
finding no way to a city for settling.
Hungry and thirsty,
their life ebbed away in them.

Then they cried out to Adonai in their trouble,
who delivered them from their distresses
and led them by a direct way
to go to a city for settling.

Let them give thanks to Adonai for unfailing love,
for deeds of wonder done
for sons and daughters of Adam and Eve,
for satisfying the throats of the thirsty
and filling the hungry with good things.

Some sit in the dark and deep gloom,
prisoners of suffering and iron,
for they rebelled against the word of El
and despised the counsel of the Most High
who subjected their heart to the bitter labor,
and no one was there to help.

Then they cried in their trouble to Adonai,
who saved them from their distresses,
brought them out from the dark and deep gloom,
and broke away their chains.

Let them give thanks to Adonai for unfailing love,
for deeds of wonder done
for sons and daughters of Adam and Eve,
for breaking down gates of bronze
and cutting through bars of iron.

Some were fools through their rebellious ways,
afflicted because of their iniquities.
Loathing all food, they drew themselves
near to the gates of death.

Then they cried in their trouble to Adonai,
who saved them from their distresses,
sending forth the word to heal them
and rescue them from their graves.

Psalm 107, continued

Let them give thanks to Adonai for unfailing love,
for deeds of wonder done
for sons and daughters of Adam and Eve,
and let them sacrifice offerings of thanksgiving
and tell of the works with songs of joy.

Some went to the sea in ships
to do trade on the mighty waters.
They saw the works in the deep,
the wonderful deeds of Adonai,
who spoke and stirred up the tempest wind
and lifted up the waves.

They mounted up to the heavens
and went down to the deep;
in peril their courage melted away.
They reeled and staggered like drunkards,
all of them at their wits end.

Then they cried in their trouble to Adonai,
who brought them out from their distresses,
stilling the storm to a whisper
and hushing the waves.
They were glad when it grew calm
and they were guided to the haven they desired.

Let them give thanks to Adonai for unfailing love,
for deeds of wonder done
for sons and daughters of Adam and Eve,
and let them exalt in the assembly of the people,
and in the council of elders give praise.

Day 22 - MORNING

Adonai turned rivers into desert,
springs of waters into thirsty ground,
and land of fruit into a salt waste
because of bad ways of those living there.

Adonai then turned desert into pools of waters,
parched ground into springs of waters,
and brought hungry ones to live there.

They founded and settled a city,
sowed fields and planted vineyards,
and yielded the fruit of harvest.
They were blessed and they increased greatly,
and their herds were not allowed to diminish.

Then they decreased and were humbled
by oppression, calamity and sorrow.
With contempt poured on them,
nobles were made to wander in a trackless waste.

But the needy were lifted from affliction
and their families increased like a flock.
The upright see this and rejoice,
but doers of the bad shut their mouth.

Whoever is wise, heed these things
and ponder the unfailing love of Adonai.

• • •

PSALM 108

Antiphon — *The one doing the truth comes to the light.* Jn 3:21

My heart is steadfast, God; I will sing
and even my soul will make music.
Awake the harp and lyre;
I will wake up the dawn!

I will praise you among the nations, Adonai,
and I will sing of you among the peoples,
for greater than above the heavens is your love
and to the skies your fidelity.

Be exalted above the heavens, God,
your glory over all the earth
that your loved ones may be delivered.
Save your right hand, and help me!

God spoke from the sanctuary:
"I will triumph and parcel out Shechem,
and measure the valley of Succoth;
mine are Gilead and Manasseh,

Ephraim my head helmet,
Judah my scepter,
and Moab my washbasin;
On Edom I toss my sandals
and over Philistia I shout in triumph."

Who will bring me to the Fortress City?
Who will lead me into Edom?
Have you, God, not rejected us,
and not gone out, God, with our armies?

Against enmity give to us aid,
for worthless is human help.
In God will we gain victory…

•

Note: Psalm 109 is omitted
in the *Liturgy of the Hours*.

PSALM 110:1-6a,7

Antiphon *Get the people to recline
in groups of about fifty.*   Lk 9:14

Adonai said to my Lord:
"Sit at my right hand
until I make enmity
as a footstool for your feet."

A scepter of your might
Adonai will extend from Zion,
and rule in the midst of enmity!

Your troops are willing on the day of your battle.
In holy majesty from the womb of the dawn,
to you is the dew of your youth.
Adonai pledged in a mind unchanging,
"You are a priest to forever
in the order of Melchizedek."

The Lord is at your right hand
and will crush rulers on the day of wrath,
will judge the nations…
and will drink from a brook on the way
with head lifted up in it all.

• • •

Day 23 - MORNING

PSALM 111

Antiphon *Stretching out his hand right away,
Jesus took hold of Simon, and said,
Little-faith, why did you doubt?*   Mt 14:31

Hallelujah!

I will extol Adonai with all my heart
in the assembled council of the upright.
Great are the works of Adonai,
pondered by all who delight in them.

Glorious and majestic are the deeds,
and this wise design endures to forever.
Remembered are the deeds of wonder
by gracious and compassionate Adonai,

providing food for ones fearing the One,
remembering the covenant to forever,
and having shown power at work,
giving the people the lands of the nations.

Faithful and just is the handiwork of Adonai,
whose precepts are worthy of trust.
Steadfast are they forever to forever,
done with fidelity and honesty.

Redemption is sent for Adonai's people;
ordained to forever is the covenant.
Holy and awesome is the Name.

Psalm 111, continued

The beginning of wisdom is fear of Adonai,
good understanding for all who live by it.
Praise endures to eternity.

•

PSALM 112

Antiphon — *Blessed are those hungering
and thirsting for justice;
they will be satisfied.* — Mt 5:6

Hallelujah!

Blessed are the ones who fear Adonai,
and delight greatly in the commandments.
Mighty in the land will they be,
blessed with generations of upright children,

wealth and riches in their houses,
and justice enduring to forever.
Light dawns in the darkness
for the upright, gracious,
compassionate and just.

The good human, generous and lending,
conducts affairs with justice.
Surely to forever the good one will not be shaken;
remembered forever will the just one be.

Day 23 - MORNING

The good will have no fear of bad news,
being steadfast of heart and trusting Adonai
with heart secure, no fear to the end,
when face to face with enmity.

The good one scatters, giving to the poor,
with justice enduring to forever;
the dignity of the good one will be lifted in honor.

Doers of the bad will see this and be vexed
with gnashing of teeth and a wasting away,
longings for the bad coming to nothing.

•

Four Ways to Pray Deeper:

↓ Talking <u>at</u> God, using memorized prayers to simply pray,
or throwing up on God today's urgency;
↓ Talking <u>to</u> God, sharing joys that are lifting my heart
and sorrows that are weighing me down;
↓ <u>Listen</u>ing to God, willing to be surprised by God who is
always saying, *I made you, I know you, I love you*;
↓ <u>Being with</u> God, contemplation, beatific vision, we can
choose to do the first three, but this is always a gift.

See *Armchair Mystic* by Mark E. Thibodeaux, S.J.

PSALM 113

Antiphon *No servant can serve two lords,*
and you cannot serve
God and mammon. Lk 16:13

Hallelujah!

Praise, you who serve Adonai!
Praise the name Adonai!

Blessed be the name of Adonai
from now and to forevermore.
From the rising of the sun to its setting
praised be the name of Adonai.

Exalted over all the nations is Adonai,
the glory above the heavens.
Who is like our God Adonai,
sitting enthroned on high,
stooping to look down
on the heavens and the earth?

Adonai raises the poor from dust
and lifts up the needy from ash heaps
to sit with royals, the royals of the people,
and settles the childless woman in a home,
a happy mother of children.

Hallelujah!

• • •

Day 23 - EVENING

PSALM 114

Antiphon *I tell you, forgive; not seven times,
           but to seventy times seven.*   Mt 18:22

When Israel came out from Egypt,
the house of Jacob
free from people of another tongue,
Judah became as God's sanctuary,
and Israel God's dominion.

The sea looked and fled, the Jordan turned back.
The mountains skipped like rams
and hills like a flock of lambs.

What to you, sea, that you fled?
Jordan, that you turned back?
Mountains, that you skipped like rams?
You hills, like a flock of lambs?

Tremble, earth, at the presences of the Lord!
Tremble at the presences of the God of Jacob,
who turned rock into pools of waters,
hard rock into springs of waters.

•

PSALM 115

Antiphon *Anyone who loves me will keep my word;*
my Abba will love that one,
within whom we will come
and make our dwelling. Jn 14:23

Not to us, **Adonai**, not to us,
but to your name give glory
because of your love, because of your fidelity.
Why say the nations, "Where now is their God?"

Our God now is in the heavens
and does all that God pleases.
Their idols are silver and gold,
made of human hands.

Made with a mouth, they cannot speak;
made with eyes, they cannot see;
made with ears, they cannot hear;
made with a nose, they cannot smell;

made with hands, they cannot feel;
made with feet, they cannot walk,
and they make not a sound in their throat.
Like them will become those who make them,
and all who trust in them.

Day 23 - EVENING

Israel, trust Adonai, your help and your shield.
Aaron, trust Adonai, your help and your shield.
You who fear Adonai, trust Adonai,
your help and your shield.

Adonai remembers us and will bless us,
will bless the house of Israel,
will bless the house of Aaron,
will bless ones who fear Adonai,
the small ones with the great ones.

May Adonai make an increase to you,
to you and to your children.
May you be blessed by Adonai,
Maker of heavens and earth.

All the heavens are the heavens of Adonai,
but earth is given to humanity.
The dead ones do not praise Adonai,
and not all those who go down in silence.

But we, we give glory to Adonai,
from now and to forevermore.
Hallelujah!

• • •

Given ten words to tell what his Mr. Jesus is about:
We are all bastards, and God loves us anyway.

See *Brother to a Dragonfly* by Will D. Campbell,
preacher, civil rights activist

PSALM 116:1-9

Antiphon *It is fitting for the Son of Humanity*
to suffer much and be rejected
and be killed, and rise after three days. Mk 8:31

I love Adonai who heard my voice
and my cries for mercy, and turned an ear to me,
so all during my days I will call.

Cords of death entangled me
and worries over Sheol came upon me;
trouble and sorrow came over me.
Then I called on the name of Adonai:
"Oh, Adonai, save my self!"

Adonai is gracious and just,
our God the compassionate one.
Adonai protects the simple hearted;
I was in need and then I was saved.

Return, my soul, to your rest,
for good to you has been Adonai,
who freed my soul from death,
my eyes from tears, and my feet from stumbling,

that I may walk before Adonai
in the land of the living.

•

PSALM 116:10-19

Antiphon *As I, the Lord and Teacher, washed your feet,*
so also are you to wash the feet of each other.

Jn 13:14

I believed it and so said, "I am greatly afflicted."
I said when it dismayed me, "Everyone is a liar."

How can I repay to Adonai
all the goodness to me?
I will lift the cup of salvation
and call on the name of Adonai.

My vows to Adonai I will now fulfill
in the presence of all the people.
Precious in the eyes of Adonai
are the saints to the death.

Adonai, I am your servant,
your servant and child of your servant;
you freed me from the chains.
I will offer the sacrifice of thanksgiving
and call on the name of Adonai.

My vows to Adonai I will now fulfill
in the presence of all the people,
in courts of the house of Adonai,
in your midst, Jerusalem.

Hallelujah!

PSALM 117

Antiphon *As the centurion responded:*
I am not worthy
for you to enter under my roof,
but only say the word
and let your servant be healed.   Lk 7:6,7

Praise Adonai, all you nations;
and give glory, all you peoples.

Great is this steadfast love toward us;
the fidelity of Adonai to forever.

Hallelujah!

•

There is an old joke that Jesus
walking around heaven asks Peter how some
folks got in, and Peter says, 'I'm doing my job boss,
but they go to the back door and your mother lets them in.'

Day 24 - MORNING

PSALM 118

Antiphon   *I am the good shepherd,
and I know mine and mine know me.*   Jn 10:14

Give thanks to Adonai who is good,
whose love is to forever.

Let Israel now declare:
the love of the Lord to forever.
Let the house of Aaron declare:
the love of the Lord to forever.
Let those who fear Adonai declare:
the love of the Lord to forever.

In anguish I cried to Adonai
who answered me with freedom.
Adonai is with me, I will not be afraid.
What can any human do to me?
Before enmity I keep this in mind:
Adonai is with me, ready to help me.

Better to take refuge in Adonai
than to trust in the human;
Better to take refuge in Adonai
than to trust in a prince.

Psalm 118, continued

All of the nations surrounded me,
indeed did they surround me;
in the name of Adonai indeed I cut them.
They swarmed around me like bees,
they crackled like thorns in a fire;
in the name of Adonai indeed I cut them.

To push back they pushed me back to fall
but Adonai came to my help.
Adonai became my strength and my song
and became to me salvation.
Shout joy and victory in your tents, you just.

Adonai's right hand does a mighty thing,
Adonai's right hand lifted high.
Adonai's right hand does a mighty thing.
I will not die; I will live
and proclaim these deeds indeed.
To chasten, Adonai let me be chastened,
but did not give me to death.

Open for me the gates of the just;
I will enter through them
and give thanks to Adonai.
This is Adonai's gate,
where just ones may enter.
I will give thanks to you for you answered me
and you became to me salvation.

The stone the builders rejected
became the cornerstone.
With Adonai this happened
and it is marvelous in our eyes.
This is the day Adonai has made;
let us rejoice and be glad in it.

Adonai, save us now!
Adonai, grant success now!
Blessed is the one coming in the name of Adonai;
We bless you from the house of Adonai.
Our El Adonai has shined light onto us.

Join with leaf branches in the festal procession
up to the horns of the altar.
To you, my God, I will give thanks.
You, my God, I will give glory.
Give thanks to Adonai who is good,
whose love is to forever.

• • •

---

*Hallel Psalms (after Hebrew for 'to praise') are
113-118, sung on major feasts such as Passover
(see Mk 14:26). Ps 136 is called the Grand Hallel.*

PSALM 119:1-8
Aleph

Antiphon   *You have heard it said,*
an eye for an eye and a tooth for a tooth;
but I say to you,
do not resist a doer of the bad.   Mt 5:38,39

Blessed are people blameless on the way,
who walk by your teaching, Adonai.
Blessed are keepers of your statutes
who seek with all their heart.

They do no wrong;
they walk in the way.
You laid down your precepts
to be obeyed with care.

Oh that my ways were steadfast
in obedience to your decrees.
Then I will have no shame
when pondering all your commands.

I will praise you with a sincere heart
so to learn your justice.
I will obey your decrees;
do not forsake me.

•

PSALM 119:9-16
Beth

Antiphon   *It has been written,*
You shall worship the Lord your God
and only your God shall you serve.   Lk 4:8

How can a young one keep the purity way?
By living as is your word.
With all my heart I seek you;
let me not stray from your commands.

I keep your word in my heart
to not sin against you.
Be praised, Adonai.
Teach me your law.

I tell with my own lips
the laws you have spoken.
I find more joy in the way of your decrees
than in the great wealth.

I meditate on your precepts
and ponder your ways.
I delight in your law
and will remember your word.

•

PSALM 119:17-24
Gimel

Antiphon
*Come yourselves privately
to a desert place
and rest a little.*   Mk 6:31

Do good to your servant;
I will live and obey your word.
Open my eyes that I may see
things of wonder in your teaching.

From this stranger on the earth
you do not hide your commands.
My soul she is rumbling all the time
with longing for your edicts.

You rebuke the arrogant with a curse,
those straying from your commands.
Free me from scorn and contempt
as I keep your decrees.

Though powers sit and talk against me
your servant will meditate on your law.
Indeed your decrees are my delight
with whom I take counsel.

•

PSALM 119:25-32
Daleth

Antiphon   *When you pray, enter your room*
and close your door
and pray to your Abba in secret.   Mt 6:6

My soul falls flat in the dust;
make me alive as is your word.
I recount my ways and you answer me;
teach me your law.

Let me understand your precepts
and I will ponder your wonders done.
My soul she is weary with sorrow;
strengthen me as is your word.

Lead me from the ways of deceit!
Your teaching gives me grace!
I choose the way of truth;
on your edicts I set my heart.

I hold fast to your decrees, Adonai;
let me not be shamed.
I run the path of your commands
for you set my heart free.

• • •

PSALM 119:33-40
He

Antiphon

*Ones who are well
have no need of a physician,
but the sick do…
I came not to call the righteous,
but sinners.*   Mt 9:12,13b

Teach me, **Adonai**, the way of your law;
to the end will I keep her.
Give me understanding to keep your teaching
and obey her with all my heart.

Lead me in the path of your commands
for I delight in them.
Turn my heart to your decrees
and away from selfish gain.

Turn my eyes from worthless things;
make me alive in your way.
Fulfill your promise to your servant
for to fear you in awe.

Take away my fear of dread
for your edicts bring the good.
See how I long for your precepts;
in your justice make me alive!

•

PSALM 119:41-48
Waw

Antiphon *The Holy Spirit, the Paraclete,
will teach you all things.*   Jn 14:26

May your merciful love come to me, Adonai,
your promised salvation.
Then will I answer my taunters
for I trust in your word.

Take not the word of truth from my mouth
for indeed I find hope in your edicts.
I will obey your teaching always
to forever and ever.

I will walk in open freedom
for I sought out your precepts.
I will speak of your decrees
before rulers without fear

for I delight in your commands
which I love,
reaching out my hands for your commands
which I love,
and I meditate on your law.

•

PSALM 119:49-56
Zayin

Antiphon   *Gather the fragments left over
so that nothing is lost.*   Jn 6:12

Remember your word to your servant
for you give me hope.
This is my comfort in affliction:
your promise she makes me alive.

Arrogance mocks me to excess;
I do not turn from your teaching.
Remembering your ancient edicts, Adonai,
I find comfort.

Indignation grabs me
for doers of bad forsake your teaching.
Your law becomes my song
in the house where I dwell.

In the night I remember your name, Adonai,
and I will keep your teaching.
This is me:
obeying your precepts.

•

PSALM 119:57-64
Heth

Antiphon   *Be ready always*
for everyone asking you a word
concerning the hope in you.   1 Ptr 3:15b

Adonai, my portion,
I promise to obey your words.
I sought your faces with all my heart.
Have mercy on me as is your promise!

I pondered my ways
and I turned my steps to your decrees.
I will hasten and not delay
to obey your commands.

Though ropes of bad things bind me
I will not forget your teaching.
I rise in the middle of the night
to give you thanks
for your just edicts.

I am a friend to all who fear you
and those keeping your precepts.

The earth she is filled
with your mercy-love, Adonai;
teach me your law!

•

PSALM 119:65-72
Teth

Antiphon   *I have come to call not the righteous,*
but sinners to conversion.   Lk 5:32

You do good to your servant, Adonai,
as is your word.
Teach me wisdom and knowledge
for I trust in your commands.

Before my affliction I went astray
but now I obey your word.
You are good and do the good;
teach me your law.

The arrogant smear on me lies;
with all my heart I keep your precepts.
Their hearts are fat and callous;
I delight in your teaching.

My affliction was good to me
so I might learn your law.
Teaching from your mouth is more precious
than vaults full of silver and gold.

• • •

PSALM 119:73-80
Yodh

Antiphon   *Give, and it will be given to you;*
           the measure you measure
           will be measured to you.   Lk 6:38

Your hands made me and formed me;
give me understanding to learn your commands.
Ones who fear you see me and rejoice
for in your word I hope.

I know, Adonai, your edicts are just;
even in affliction you are faithful to me.
May your mercy-love now comfort me
as is your promise to your servant.

Let your compassions keep me alive,
as your teaching is my delight.
May arrogance be shamed
in wronging me without cause.
I will meditate on your precepts.

May those who fear you turn to me,
those understanding your decrees.
May my heart be all about your law
that I may be free of shame.

•

PSALM 119:81-88
Kaph

Antiphon *Cast all your anxiety on God,
to whom everything about you matters.* 1 Ptr 5:7

My soul she longs for your salvation;
in your word I put my hope.
My eyes fail searching for your promise
to say "When will you comfort me?"

Though like a wineskin dry in smoke,
I do not forget your law.
Where are the days of your servant?
When will you act on my persecutors?

The arrogant dig pitfalls for me
and not as are your teachings.
All your commands are trustworthy.
They chase me without cause; help me!

They almost wiped me from the earth
but I did not forsake your precepts.
As is your mercy-love, preserve me alive
and I will obey the decrees of your mouth.

•

PSALM 119:89-96
Lamedh

Antiphon *God saw all that God made
and found it very good.*   Genesis 1:31a

To eternity, Adonai,
your word stands firm in the heavens.
To generation and generation is your fidelity;
the earth you established endures.

Your edicts endure the day
for all things are your servants.
If your teaching were not my delight
I would have perished in my affliction.

I will never forget your precepts
for by them you make me alive.
I am yours; save me
for I sought out your precepts.

Wicked ones wait to destroy me
but I will ponder your decrees.
I see a limit to all perfection
but your commands are without boundary.

•

PSALM 119:97-104
Mem

Antiphon *Who do people say I am?*
Who do you say I am?   Mk 8:27,29

How I love your teachings,
my meditation all day long.
Your commands make me wiser than enmity
for they are with me to forever.

Greater than all my teachers is my insight
for I ponder your decrees.
I understand more than elders
for I obey your precepts.

I keep my feet off every evil path
to obey your word.
I turn not from your edicts
for you have taught me.

How sweet to my taste are your promises,
sweeter than honey to my mouth.
I gain understanding from your precepts
for I hate every false path.

• • •

Day 26 - MORNING

PSALM 119:105-112
Nun

Antiphon　　*Every scribe*
discipled to the reign of heaven
is like a head of a household
who puts forth from the treasure
things both new and old.　　Mt 13:52

Your word is the lamp to my foot
and the light for my path.
I have made an oath and confirmation
to follow your just edicts.

I have suffered much, Adonai;
make me alive as is your word.
Accept the willing praise of my mouth!
And now, Adonai, teach me your decrees!

My life is constantly in my hand,
but I will not forget your teaching.
Doers of the bad set a snare for me,
but I did not stray from your precepts.

I have your decrees as a heritage to forever,
they are indeed the joy of my heart.
I set my heart to keep your law
to forever, the very end.

●

PSALM 119:113-120
Samekh

Antiphon *Joy in heaven over one sinner repenting*
will exceed that over
ninety-nine of the righteous
with no need of repentance. Lk 15:7

I hate double-minded hypocrisy
but love your teaching.
My refuge and my shield,
in your word I put my hope.

Go away from me, doers of badness,
that I may keep my God's commands.
Sustain me as is your promise
and I will live.
Disappoint me not in my hope.

Hold me up and I will be delivered
and contemplate always your law.
You reject those who stray from your statutes
for vain is their deceit.

As dross you discard bad doers of earth
so I love your decrees.
My flesh trembles in fear of you;
I stand in awe of your edicts.

●

Day 26 - MORNING

PSALM 119:121-128
Ayin

Antiphon *Unless the grain of wheat*
falling to the ground dies,
it remains one grain;
but if it dies, it bears much fruit.   Jn 12:24

I have done justice;
abandon me not to oppression.
Ensure the welfare of your servant;
let not the arrogance oppress me.

My eyes long to see your salvation
and the promise of your justice.
Deal with your servant as is your mercy
and teach me your law.

I am your servant, give me discernment
to understand your decrees.
They disobey your teaching;
it is time for Adonai to act.

For this I love your commands
more than gold, even pure gold;
for this I follow your precepts:
I hate every wrong path.

●

PSALM 119:129-136
Pe

Antiphon *When I am lifted up from the earth,
I will draw everyone to myself.*   Jn 12:32

Your statutes are wonderful;
I myself obey them.
Your words enter giving light
and understanding to the simple.

I open my mouth and breathe heavy,
longing for your commands.
Turn to me and have mercy
as is your custom with lovers of your name.

Direct my footsteps by your word;
prevent sin from ruling over me.
Redeem me from human oppression
that I may obey your precepts.

Shine your faces on your servant
and teach me your decrees.
Streams of tears flow down my eyes
over disobedience to your teaching.

●

PSALM 119:137-144
Sadhe I

Antiphon *There are last ones who will be first*
and first ones who will be last.   Lk 13:30

You are just, Adonai,
and just are your edicts.
You laid down your decrees
in justice and full fidelity.

My zeal wears me out
for enmity ignores your words.
Your promise is tested by fire
and your servant loves her.

Belittled and despised,
I remember your precepts.
Your justice is right to everlasting
and your teaching is true.

Trouble and distress came upon me;
your commands are my delights.
Just are your decrees to forever;
give me understanding that I may live.

• • •

PSALM 119:145-152
Sadhe II

Antiphon *Ask and it will be given you,*
seek and you will find,
knock and it will be opened to you. Lk 11:9

I call with all my heart: answer me, Adonai;
your law I will obey.
I call to you: save me,
and I will keep your decrees.

I rise before dawn and I cry for help;
in your word I put my hope.
My eyes stay open in the night watch
to meditate on your promise.

Hear my voice, as you are loving, Adonai,
as your edict makes me alive.
Scheming devisers are near,
but they are far from your teaching.

You are near, Adonai,
and all your commands are true.
I learned long ago from your decrees
that you established them to forever.

•

Day 26 - EVENING

PSALM 119:153-160
Resh

Antiphon   *When coming, the Spirit of truth
will guide you into all truth.*   Jn 16:13

Look upon my affliction and deliver me
for your teaching I have not forgotten.
Defend my cause and redeem me
as your promise makes me alive!

Salvation is far from doers of the bad
who do not seek out your edicts.
Your compassions are great, Adonai,
as your edicts make me alive.

Many persecute me in enmity;
still I turn not from your decrees.
I look with perplexion on the faithless
who do not obey your word.

See how I love your precepts, Adonai,
as your mercy-love keeps me alive.
All your word is true
and to all eternity, your law of justice.

•

PSALM 119:161-168
Shin

Antiphon *Give them food yourselves.* Lk 9:13a

Rulers persecute me for no reason
but at your word my heart trembles.
I rejoice in your promise
like one finding great spoil.

I hate and abhor falsehood;
it is your teaching I love.
Seven times daily I praise you
for your edicts are just.

Great peace comes to lovers of your teaching;
they do not stumble.
I wait for your salvation, Adonai;
I follow your commands.

My self she obeys your decrees,
for greatly do I love them.
I obey your precepts and statutes
for all my ways are before you.

•

*God does not ask us to be worthy but to be
willing; it is the mercy of God that makes us worthy.*
Anthony Zoghby, Our Lady of the Gulf, Gulf Shores Alabama

Day 26 - EVENING

PSALM 119:169-176
Taw

Antiphon
*Do you believe
because you have seen me?
Blessed are those not seeing
but believing.*   Jn 20:29

May my cry come before you, Adonai,
as your word gives me understanding!
May my prayer come before you;
deliver me as you promise!

May praise out of my lips ever flow
for you teach me your law.
May my tongue sing your word
of all your just commands.

May your hand be a help to me
for your precepts I have chosen.
I long for your salvation, Adonai,
and your teaching is my delight.

Let my soul live that she may praise you;
may your edicts sustain me.
I wandered like one lost sheep.
Seek your servant
for I forget not your commands.

• • •

PSALM 120

Antiphon
*The Son of Humanity
did not come to be served
but to serve,
to give his life
in ransom for the many.* Mk 10:45

In my distress I call on Adonai who answers me.
Adonai, save my self from lips of the lie
and from the deceitful tongue.

What will be done to you and what more
will be done to you, deceiful tongue?
Arrows of war made sharp
with coals of broom trees.

Woe to me, an alien in Meshech,
living among tents of Kedar.

Too long has my self lived
among haters of peace.
I am of peace, but when I speak
they are for war.

•

Day 27 - MORNING

PSALM 121

Antiphon *When coming, will the Son of Humanity find faith on earth?* Lk 18:8

I lift up my eyes to the mountains.
From where does my help come?
My help comes from Adonai,
Maker of heavens and earth,

who will not let your foot slip
nor slumber when guarding you.
Indeed the guardian of Israel
will not slumber and will not sleep.

Adonai is your guardian,
the Most High at your right hand.
By day the sun will not harm you,
nor the moon by the night.

Adonai will keep you from all harm
and guard your life.
Adonai will guard your going and coming
from now and to forevermore.

•

---

*I think I'll just
let the mystery be.*
Iris DeMent, songwriter

PSALM 122

Antiphon *Amen, you will be with me
in paradise.* Lk 23:43

I rejoiced with those saying to me,
"Let us go to the house of Adonai."
Our feet stand in your gates, Jerusalem.

Jerusalem is built like a city
formed together, a compact.
There the tribes go up, the tribes of Adonai.

Make it in Israel a statute
to praise the name of Adonai,
for there stand the thrones of justice,
the thrones of the house of David.

Pray for the peace of Jerusalem!
May those who love you be secure.
May peace be within your walls,
security within your citadels.

For the sake of my sisters and brothers and friends
I will say, "Now, peace be within you."
For the sake of the house of our God Adonai
I will seek your prosperity.

•

Day 27 - MORNING

PSALM 123

Antiphon *Talitha koun;*
little girl, I say to you, arise. Mk 5:41

I lift up my eyes to you,
sitting in the heavens.
As eyes of a servant are
to the hand of a master,

as the eyes of a maid
are to the hand of a mistress,
see, our eyes are to Adonai
till our God shows to us mercy.

Have mercy on us, Adonai, have mercy on us,
for we have endured much contempt.
Much ridicule from proud ones
and contempt of arrogant ones
have we ourselves endured.

•

Consider what it means to
be a baptized follower of Jesus:
Lifegiver Priest, Soldier Prophet,
Footwasher Royal, and Beloved Lover.
See *God's Ones* by Stephen Joseph Wolf

PSALM 124

Antiphon *One finding one's own life will lose it,*
and one losing one's own life for my sake
will find it.   Mt 10:39

If Adonai was not for us, let Israel now say,
if Adonai was not for us
when human beings attacked against us,
then they would have swallowed us alive
when their anger blazed against us.

Then the floods would have engulfed us,
the torrents would have swept over our selfs,
and the raging waters would have swept over us.

Praise be to Adonai,
who did not let us be torn by their teeth.
Our selfs, like a bird,
escaped from the snare of fowlers.

The snare being broken we escaped.
Our help is in the name of Adonai,
the Maker of heavens and earth.

•

Take off your sandals… Offer whatever still-incomplete
awareness of illusions that you can… Then let Jesus pray…
See *Too Deep For Words* by Thelma Hall

Day 27 - MORNING

PSALM 125

Antiphon *If you know to give good gifts to your children,
how much more will the heavenly Abba
give the Holy Spirit to all who ask.*   Lk 11:13

They who trust in Adonai are like Mount Zion;
not to be shaken, they endure to forever.

As mountains surround around Jerusalem,
so Adonai surrounds around the people
from now and to forevermore.

Indeed the sceptor of bad doings
will not remain over the lot of the just
lest the hands of the just be used for the bad.

Do good, Adonai, to the good,
even to those honest in their hearts!
But those who turn to bad ways
Adonai will banish with doers of the bad.

Peace be upon Israel!

• • •

---

*A salty parish priest retiring to his
home town made sandwiches to give away
in a park. Cash that another priest sent to help was
returned with a note, 'Make your own damn sandwiches.'*

PSALM 126

Antiphon *What do you wish me to do for you?*
...Go, your faith has healed you. Mk 10:51,52

When Adonai restored Zion out of captivity
we felt like people in a dream.
Then our mouth was filled with laughter,
and our tongue with a song of joy.

Then they said among the nations
"Their Adonai did great things for them."
Adonai did great things for us;
we were full of joy.

Restore our good fortune, Adonai,
like streams in the Negev desert.
Sowers are now in tears;
they will reap with a song of joy.

Going out, the sower goes out weeping,
carrying seeds for the sowing.
Returning, the sower will return
carrying sheaves with a song of joy.

•

*God our Savior desires that all
humans be saved and come to know the truth.*
1 Timothy 2:3b,4

PSALM 127

Antiphon *Look at the birds of heaven and see:*
they do not sow or reap or gather into barns
and your heavenly Abba feeds them.   Mt 6:26

If Adonai does not build the house,
the builders labor in vanity.
If Adonai does not watch over the city,
the watcher stands guard in vain.

It is vanity to rise early or stay up late,
or to eat the bread of hard toil;
the Lord provides as the beloved get their sleep.

See, heritage of Adonai!
Sons are a reward, and daughters of the womb.
Like arrows in the hand of a warrior,
so are children of one's youth.

Blessed are they whose quivers are full of them;
they will not be shamed
when they speak with enmity at the gate.

•

The Catechism…says that Catholics are called to treat
(LGBTQIA+ people) with respect, compassion, and sensitivity.
See *Building a Bridge* by James Martin, SJ, CCC #2358

PSALM 128

Antiphon *Everyone having will be given more
and to abundance; but the one not having,
even that will be taken.* Mt 25:29

Blessed are all who fear Adonai
and walk in the way.

Indeed you will eat from the labor of your hands.
To you will be blessings and prosperity,
and your spouse like a fruitful vine
inside and outside your house,
sons and daughters around your table
like shoots of the olives.

See: one who fears Adonai is blessed;
may Adonai bless you from Zion.
See and enjoy the prosperity of Jerusalem
all the days of your life,
and the joy of the children of your children.

Peace be upon Israel.

•

*You sanctify
whatever you are grateful for.*
Anthony de Mello, Jesuit

PSALM 129

Antiphon *I am the bread of life; who comes to me does not hunger and who believes in me will never thirst.*   Jn 6:35

"**From my youths** they oppressed me greatly,"
let Israel now say.
"From my youths they oppressed me greatly,
but gained no victory over me.

On my back the plowers plowed;
long are the furrows they made.
Adonai the Just
cut free the cords of bad doings."

May all haters of Zion
be shamed and turned back;
May they be like grass on housetops
which withers before it grows,

which cannot fill one hand of the reaper
nor an arm of the gatherer,
and passers-by will not say,
"Blessing of Adonai upon you!
We bless you in the name of Adonai!"

•

PSALM 130

Antiphon *Whoever does the will of God
is my brother and sister and mother.*   Mk 3:35

Out of the depths I cry to you, Adonai.
Lord, hear my voice.
Let your ears be attentive to my cries for mercy.

If you kept a record of sins, Adonai,
Lord, who could stand?
But with you is the forgiveness,
and so you are revered in awe.

I wait, my soul waits for Adonai,
in whose word I put hope.
My soul waits for the Lord
more than watchers for the morning,
even watchers for the morning.

Put hope, Israel, in Adonai!
For unfailing love is from Adonai,
in whom is full redemption,
who will redeem Israel from all their sins.

●

*The glory of God is
the human person fully alive.*
Saint Irenaeus, d. 202

Day 27 - EVENING

PSALM 131

Antiphon *Scribes and Pharisees*
preach and do not do it;
they put on human shoulders
heavy burdens bound,
but are unwilling
to lift a finger to move them.   Mt 23:3b,4

Adonai, my heart is not proud
and my eyes are not haughty
and I am not busied with the great matters,
with things so wonderful as to be beyond me.

But indeed I have become still
and quiet in my soul
like a child with a mother, being weaned.
Like one being weaned is my soul within me.

Israel, put your hope in Adonai
from now and to forevermore.

• • •

As a child rests in
their mother's arms, this is
how my soul rests in you, O God.

God uses parents to reveal to children something (not everything, but something) about who God is.

PSALM 132

Antiphon *To the one who has, more will be given;*
from the one who has not,
even what that one has
will be taken away.   Mk 4:25

Adonai, remember David
and all the hardships he endured,
the oath he swore to Adonai,
the vow he made to the Mighty One of Jacob.

I will not enter into the structure of my house;
I will not go to the mats of my bed;
I will not allow my eyes to sleep
nor let slumber come to my eyelids,
till I find a place for Adonai,
a dwelling for the Mighty One of Jacob.

See, we heard her in Ephrathah;
we came upon her in fields of Jaar.
"Let us go to the dwellings;
let us worship at the feet on the footstool."

Arise, Adonai, to your rest,
you and the ark of your might.
May your priests be clothed with justice
and may your saints sing for joy.

For the sake of your servant David
reject not the face of your anointed one.

Adonai swore an oath to David,
sure and not to be revoked.
"From the descendants of your body
I will place on your throne.

If your sons and daughters keep my covenant
and my statutes that I teach them
then their children to forever
will sit on your throne."

For Adonai chose Zion
and desired her as a dwelling:
"This is my resting place to forever;
here I will sit, for I desired her.

To bless I will bless her provisions;
her poor ones I will satisfy with food,
her priests I will clothe in salvation,
and her saints will sing; they will sing for joy.

Here I will sprout a horn for David;
I will set up a lamp for my anointed one.
Enmity will be clothed with shame.
The crown on David will be resplendent."

•

God has given us all these wonderful toys;
ought we not to play with them?   Sister Wendy Beckett

PSALM 133

Antiphon *The multitude of believers
was heart and soul one.* Acts 4:32a

See how good and how pleasant it is
to live as siblings
dwelling in unity.

Like the precious oil
running down on the head
and on the beard of Aaron,
running down on his collar and robes,

as if the dew of Hermon
was falling on Mount Zion,
there Adonai bestows
the blessing of life to forever.

•

*The
primary
addiction is
addiction to self,
plain old selfishness.*
Fr Phillip Breen

Day 28 - MORNING

PSALM 134

Antiphon	*Be not afraid.*	Mt 10:26, 14:27, 17:17, 28:10,…; Mk 6:50,…; Lk 5:10, 12:4,…; Jn 6:20,…

See Adonai and give praise,
all you servants of Adonai,
and ministers at night in the house of Adonai.

Lift up your hands in the sanctuary
and praise Adonai!

May Adonai bless you from Zion,
the One Maker of heavens and the earth.

•

Somebody
went to the bother of
counting the number of
times that "be not afraid" is
found in the Bible. How many?
Once for each day of the year: 365

PSALM 135

Antiphon *What is the profit for a human to gain
the whole world but lose their life?* Mt 16:26

Hallelujah! Praise the name of Adonai!
Servants of Adonai, give praise!
You who minister in the house of Adonai,
in the courts of the house of our God,

praise Adonai, for good is Adonai!
Sing praise to the Name, for it is pleasant!
Adonai has chosen Jacob,
Israel the chosen treasure.

For I know that great is our Lord;
greater than all the "gods" is Adonai,
who does as Adonai pleases
in the heavens and on earth and in the deep sea,

making clouds rise from the ends of the earth,
sending lightning with the rain,
and bringing wind from the storehouses,

who struck down the firstborn of Egypt,
from human to animals,
sending signs and wonders to the midst of Egypt
against Pharaoh and against all of his servants,

having struck down
many nations and mighty rulers: -

Day 28 - MORNING

Sihon, rulers of the Amorites, and Og of Bashan,
and all the rulers of Canaan,
who gave their land as an inheritance,
an inheritance to Israel, the people of Adonai.

Your name, Adonai, is to forever,
your renown to generation and generation,
for you, Adonai, will vindicate your people
and will have compassion on your servants.

Idols of the nations are silver and gold,
the work of human hands.
A mouth to them but they cannot speak.
Eyes to them but they cannot see.

Ears to them but they cannot hear,
and there is no breath in their mouth.
Like them will be their makers
and all who trust in them.

House of Israel, praise Adonai!
House of Aaron, praise Adonai!
House of Levi, praise Adonai!
You who fear Adonai, praise Adonai!

Praised be Adonai from Zion,
dwelling in Jerusalem.
Hallelujah!

• • •

PSALM 136

Antiphon *My food is that I may do the will*
of the one who sent me. Jn 4:34

Give thanks to Adonai who is good,
loving to forever.
Give thanks to the One who is El of the "els,"
loving to forever.
Give thanks to the One who is Lord of the lords,
loving to forever,

to the One who has alone done great wonders,
who made the heavens by understanding,
who spread out the earth upon the waters,
loving to forever,

who made the great lights,
the sun to govern the day,
the moon and stars to govern the night,
loving to forever,

who struck down Egypt in their firstborn,
who brought Israel out from among them,
with mighty hand and outstretched arm,
loving to forever,

who divided the Reed Sea in half,
and brought Israel through its midst,
but swept Pharoah and the army
into the Reed Sea,
loving to forever,

who then led the people through the desert,
who struck down great rulers,
and killed mighty rulers,
loving to forever,

Sihon, king of the Amorites,
and Og, the king of Bashan,
loving to forever,

who gave the land as an inheritance,
an inheritance to servant Israel,
who remembered us in our low estate,
loving to forever,

and freed us from enmity,
who gives food to every creature.
Give thanks to El of the heavens,
who indeed is loving to forever!

•

Lord, take me where you want me to go;
let me meet who you want me to meet;
tell me what you want me to say;
and keep me out of your way.

Lord Take Me by Mychal Judge, OFM

Name of God

Adonai *is
Hebrew for "My
Lord."* **YHVH**, *is
usually translated
LORD in all caps, for
most faithful Jews would
not speak the name Yahweh,
but instead would say Adonai.
Yhvh is the name revealed to Moses at
the burning bush, and means 'I am who
I am,' or 'I will be who I will be,' or simply
'I am.'* **El** *can mean any god, remembering that
nations and cities would have their own gods. The
plural for El is* **Elohim***, which can mean many gods,
but in the psalms refers to the one Yhvh without any
sense of being multiple gods.* **El Shaddai** *(God Almighty)
is how the Patriarchs spoke of the one God.* **Yhvh Sabaoth**
(Lord of Hosts) refers to God enthroned with an army of angels.

PSALM 137:1-6

Antiphon *God so loved the cosmos,*
and so gave the only begotten Son that
everyone believing in him may not perish
but have eternal life.   Jn 3:16

By rivers of Babylon, there we sat and wept
as we remembered Zion;
On the poplars in their midst we hung our harps,

for there our captors asked us for words of song,
our tormentors for joy:
"Sing for us from the songs of Zion!"

How can we sing in a foreign land
a song of Adonai?
If I forget you, Jerusalem,
may my right hand forget its skill.

May my tongue cling to the roof of my mouth
if I remember you not,
if I consider any but Jerusalem
as the height of my joy.

•

Scholars suggest that what we know as the Pentateuch, the
first five books, the Torah, were edited 2,500 years ago in the
Babylonian Exile, not knowing if they would return to Jerusalem.

PSALM 138

Antiphon   *Put out into the deep
and let down your nets for a catch.*   Lk 5:4

I will praise you, **Adonai**, with all my heart.
Before those so-called "gods"
I will sing my praise of you.
I will bow toward your holy temple
and I will praise your name
for your love and your fidelity.

You are exalted above all,
your name and your word.
On the day I called, then you answered me.
You made me bold and stout in my heart.

May all the rulers of the earth praise you, Adonai,
when they hear the words of your mouth.
May they sing of the ways of Adonai,
for great is the glory of Adonai.

Though on high, Adonai looks upon the lowly
and knows the proud from afar.
Though I walk in the midst of trouble,
you keep me alive
against the anger of enmity.

Day 28 - EVENING

You stretch out your hand, your right hand,
and you save me.
Adonai will fulfill me.
Your love, Adonai, is to forever.
Abandon not the works of your hands.

• • •

PSALM 139:1-18,23-24

Antiphon *To you hearing I say,*
love your enemies
and do good to the ones hating you. Lk 6:27

Adonai, you search me and you know me.
You know my sitting and my rising;
you perceive my thoughts from afar.
You mark my going and my lying down,
and you are familiar with all of my ways.

When a word is not yet on my tongue
you see it, Adonai; you know them all.
Behind and before you hem me in
and rest your hand upon me.
Too wonderful for me is this knowledge,
more lofty than what I can attain.

Where can I hide from your Spirit?
Where could I flee from your presences?
If I go up to the heavens, you are there;
if I make a bed in Sheol, you I see!

If I rise on the wings of dawn,
if I settle on the far side of the sea,
even there your hand will guide me
and your right hand will hold me…

Day 29 - MORNING

If I say, "Surely darkness will hide me
and the night will light around me,"
even darkness will not be dark to you
and night will shine as the day;
as the darkness, so the light.

For you created my inmost beings;
you knit me together in my mother's womb.
I praise you because I am full of fear and wonder;
my self knows well
how wonderful are your works.

My bones were not hidden from you
when I was made in the secret place,
woven together in the depths of earth.

Your eyes saw my body
and in your book were written and ordained
all the days before the first day was.

How precious to me, El, are your designs,
how vast are they, the sums of them;
if countable they number more than the sand.
Awake and still, I am with you.

Search me, El, and know my heart!
Test me, and know my anxious thoughts!
See if there is in me an offensive way,
then lead me in the way everlasting!

•

PSALM 140:1-9,13-14

Antiphon *Blessed are you when they disrespect*
and persecute and tell all the lies
against you for my sake;
rejoice and be glad,
for great is your reward
in the heavens.   Mt 5:11

Day 29 - MORNING

Rescue me, Adonai,
from humans doing bad things;
protect me from humans of violence
who devise the bad in their hearts
and stir up conflict every day.
They make their tongues sharp as a serpent;
viper poison is on their lips.

Keep me, Adonai, from their hands;
protect me from humans of violence
who plan to trip up my feet.
Arrogance has hidden a snare for me,
spread a net of cords,
and set a trap for me beside the path.

I say to Adonai, "You are my God!"
Hear, Adonai, the cry of my cries for mercy!
Lord Adonai, my strength, my deliverance,
you shield my head on the day of battle.
Grant not, Adonai, their desires;
let not their plans to do the bad succeed…

I know that Adonai secures justice for the poor
and the cause of the needy.
Surely the just will praise your Name;
the upright will live before your faces.

• • •

PSALM 141

Antiphon *Blessed are the merciful,*
for they will receive mercy.   Mt 5:7

The Beatitudes   Mt 5:3-12
Blessed are the poor in spirit,
for theirs is the reign of heaven.
Blessed are those mourning,
for they will be comforted.
Blessed are the meek,
for they will inherit the earth.
Blessed are those hungering and thirsting
for justice, for they will be satisfied.
Blessed are the merciful,
for they will receive mercy.
Blessed are the clean of heart,
for they will see God.
Blessed are the peacemakers,
for they will be called children of God.
Blessed are those who are persecuted for what is right,
for theirs is the reign of heaven.
Blessed are you when they disrespect and persecute
and tell all the lies against you for my sake;
rejoice and be glad, for great is your reward in the heavens.

Day 29 - EVENING

Adonai, I call to you; be quick to come to me.
Hear my voice when I call to you.
May my prayer be as incense set before you,
lifting my hands in evening sacrifice.

Set guard, Adonai, over my mouth.
Keep watch over the gate of my lips.
Let my heart not be drawn to evil matter,
to join in bad deeds with their doers
or to eat of their delicacies.

Let the just person strike me, a kindness,
and rebuke me, as oil on my head;
my head will not refuse this,
my prayer is ever against bad deeds.

Their rulers will drop over cliff edge;
they will learn that my words were well spoken:
"As a farmer breaks up the earth,
bones were scattered at the mouth of Sheol."

But on you, Lord Adonai, are my eyes,
and in you I take refuge;
do not give my self over to death.

Keep me from the hands of the snares
and from the traps of those doing the bad.
When they fall together into their nets,
keep me in safety.

•

*Life is a mystery to be lived,
not a problem to be solved.*
Soren Kierkegaard

PSALM 142

Antiphon *Let the light of you shine before humanity,*
that they may see your good works
and give glory to your Abba in heaven.

Mt 5:16

My voice cries to Adonai;
my voice asks for mercy from Adonai,
before whom I pour out my complaint,
before whom I tell my trouble.
When my spirit grows faint within me
then you know my way.

In the path where I walk they hid a snare for me.
Look right and see: the one with concern for me
has fled away from me for refuge;
there is no one who cares for my life.

I cry to you, Adonai, and say you are my refuge,
my portion in the land of the living.
Listen, El, to my cry, for I am in desperate need.

Rescue me from the strong ones pursuing me;
set my self free from prison to praise your name.
The just ones will gather about me
because you are good to me.

•

PSALM 143:1-11

Antiphon *Go into all the cosmos and
proclaim the gospel to all creation.* Mk 16:15

Adonai, hear my prayer.
Listen in your fidelity to my cries for mercy.
Relieve me in your justice.
Bring not your servant into judgment
for not anyone alive is just before you.

Indeed enmity pursues my self
and crushes my life to the ground
and makes me dwell in dark places
like dead ones of long ago.
My spirit grows faint within me;
within me my heart is dismayed.

I remember days of long ago
and meditate on all of your work
and consider the deeds of your hands.
I stretch out my hands to you;
like land parched my soul thirsts for you.

Be quick! Answer me, Adonai! My spirit faints!
Hide not your faces from me
or I will be like and with ones going down the pit.

Bring in the morning your word of unfailing love,
for in you I trust.
Show me the way I should go
for to you I lift up my soul!

Rescue me, Adonai, from enmity; in you I hide.
Teach me to do your will, for you are my El.
May your good Spirit lead me on level ground.

For the sake of your Name, Adonai,
you keep me alive in your justice;
you bring my self out from trouble.

• • •

Abba, you call us to the table of your Son,
renew us by word and sacrament,
and send us to labor in your harvest.
We are a people in need of the witness
of faithful marriages and priests,
generous single people and deacons,
religious sisters, brothers, monks and nuns.
Help each disciple to trust in your call,
make us able and willing to do what you ask,
keep us united in our gifted diversity,
and bring to maturity every seed you sow.
All this we ask through the Good Shepherd:
Jesus Christ, your Son and our Lord.

PSALM 144

Antiphon *Zaccheus, come down quickly,*
for this day it is fitting
for me to stay at your house. Lk 19:5

Praised be Adonai, my Rock,
who trains my hands for war, my fingers for battle,

my love and fortress, my stronghold and deliverer,
my shield in whom I take refuge,
who subdues peoples under me.

What, Adonai, is a human, that you care for us?
Children of humanity, that you think of them?
Like a breath is the human,
whose days are like a shadow passing.

Adonai, part your heavens and come down!
Touch the mountains so they smoke!
You send lightning lit to scatter enmity!
Shoot your arrows and you rout them!

Reach your hands from on high!
Deliver me! Rescue me from the mighty waters,
from the hand of foreign peoples speaking lies
whose right hands are the right hand of deceit.

I will sing a new song to you, God,
and on the lyre of ten make music to you,
the One giving victory to the rulers,
the One delivering your servant David
from the deadly sword.

Deliver me! Rescue me from foreign hands,
whose mouths speak the lie,
whose right hands are the right hand of deceit.

Our children in their youth
are like well nurtured plants,
like carved pillars adorning a palace,

our barns filled with provisions of every kind,
our sheep becoming thousands
and tens of thousands in our fields,
and our oxen drawing loads,

no break in the walls and no exile
nor a cry of distress in the streets:
Blessed are the people of whom all this is true;
blessed are the people whose God is Adonai.

•

PSALM 145

Antiphon *The Son of Humanity came
to seek and to save the lost.* Lk 19:10

I will exalt you, my God the Ruler,
and I will praise your Name to forever.

In every day I will praise you
and I will bless your Name to forever.
Great is Adonai, and greatly being praised,
an unfathomable greatness.

Generation to generation commend your works
and tell of your mighty acts
and the glorious splendor of your majesty,
and I will meditate on your wonderful deeds.

They will tell of your awesome works
and I will proclaim your great deeds.
They will celebrate and remember
the abundance of your goodness
and they will sing of your justice.

Gracious and compassionate is Adonai,
slow to anger, rich in love, and good to all.
Adonai's compassion is on every creature.

All your works will praise you, Adonai,
and your saints will bless you.
They will tell of the glory of your reign
and speak your might to make known

Day 30 - MORNING

to sons and daughters of humanity your acts
and the glorious splendor of your reign,
the realm of all the ages,
and your dominion through all
generation and generation.

Adonai is faithful to all the promises
and loving to all who are made.
Adonai upholds all who are falling
and lifts up all who are bowed down.

The eyes of all look to you
and you give them their food in due season,
opening your hand and satisfying the desire
of every living thing.

Just is Adonai in all ways,
and loving to all who are made.
Near is Adonai to all who call,
to all who call in truth.

Fulfilled is the desire
of all who fear and love Adonai,
who hears their cry and saves them
and watches over them.
But bad ways will be destroyed.

My mouth will speak praise of Adonai.
Let every creature praise the holy Name
to forever and ever.

•

PSALM 146

Antiphon *Blessed are the meek,
for they will inherit the earth.* Mt 5:5

Hallelujah!

Praise Adonai, my soul!
I will praise Adonai during my life;
I will sing praise to my God while I still am.

Trust neither royalty nor human beings
in whom there is no salvation.
Their spirit-breath departs,
and they return to the ground.
On that day their plans come to nothing.

Blessed are they whose help is the God of Jacob,
whose hope and God are Adonai,
the maker of heaven and earth
and the sea and all that is in them.

The one staying faithful to forever
defends justice for the oppressed
and gives food to the hungry.

Adonai sets prisoners free;
Adonai gives sight to the blind;
Adonai lifts those who are bowed down;
Adonai loves the just.

Day 30 - MORNING

Adonai watches over alien strangers,
and sustains the orphan and the widow,
but frustrates the ways that are bad.
Adonai reigns to forever,
your God, Zion,
from generation to generation.

Hallelujah!

• • •

God has
distributed gifts
and blessings in such
a way that every person
has a particular place and
purpose within society—and
thus everyone is equally necessary
for a society to function well...
How wonderful it would be if villages
and towns could become like large families.
Then heaven would come down to earth.

See *On Living Simply: the Golden Voice of John Chrysostom*
edited by Robert Van de Weyer

PSALM 147

Antiphon   *I am the living bread from heaven;*
anyone who eats of this bread
will live to the eon.   Jn 6:51a

Hallelujah!
How good it is to sing praise to our God!
How pleasant and fitting to give praise!

Adonai rebuilds Jerusalem, gathers Israel's exiles,
heals broken hearts and binds up wounds,
determines the number of the stars,
and calls to each of them by name.

Great and mighty in power is our Lord,
with unlimited understanding.
Adonai sustains the humble
and throws doers of the bad to the dust.
Sing to Adonai with thanksgiving!

Make music on the harp to our God,
who covers the skies with clouds
and supplies rain to the earth,
making grass to grow on the mountains,
providing food for cattle
and young ravens when they call.

Day 30 - EVENING

Adonai finds pleasure
not in the strength of the horse
nor delight in the legs of the human,
but is delighting in those who fear Adonai
who hope in this unfailing love.

Glorify Adonai, Jerusalem!
Zion, now give praise!

Your God strengthens the bars of your gates,
blesses your peoples within you,
brings peace to your border,
and satisfies you with finest of wheat.

Your God sends a command to the earth,
and swiftly runs a word,
spreading snow like the wool
and scattering frost like the ash.

Hail is hurled like pebbles;
who can stand before the icy blast?
The word of the Lord is sent, and they melt;
wind stirs up and the waters flow.

The word of the Lord is revealed to Jacob,
decrees and laws of the Lord to Israel.
Not for another nation did the Lord do this;
they do not know these laws.
Hallelujah!

•

PSALM 148

Antiphon *This I command,
that you love one another.* Jn 15:17

Hallelujah!

Give praise from the heavens!
Give praise in the heights.
Give praise all you angels.
Give praise all you hosts.

Give praise sun and moon.
Give praise all stars shining.
Give praise, you heavens of the heavens
and waters above the heavens.

Let them praise the name Adonai,
who commanded and they were created,
who set them in place forever,
to forever the decree Adonai gave,
not to pass away.

Praise Adonai, you earth,
you sea creatures and all in the deep,
lightning and hail, snow and cloud,
wind of the storm, all who do Adonai's bidding,

Day 30 - EVENING

you mountains and hills,
fruit trees and cedars,
wild animals and all cattle,
small creatures and birds of flight,

you rulers of the earth and the nations,
royals and all people ruling on earth,
young men and young women,
old folks and children:

Let them praise the name Adonai
whose name alone is exalted,
whose splendor is above earth and the heavens,

who raised a horn for the people,
praise of all the saints,
of the sons and daughters of Israel,
of people close to the Lord.

Hallelujah!

•

Grace wakes us up when we're ready.
Sr. Helen Prejean, October 28, 2011

PSALM 149:1-6,9c

Antiphon *John the Baptist told his disciples, this joy of mine is full; it is fitting for the Christ to increase and for me to decrease.* Jn 3:30

Hallelujah!

Sing to Adonai a new song,
praise in the assembly of saints.
Let Israel rejoice in their Maker,
let the people of Zion be glad in their ruler.

Let them praise the name
with dance, tambourine and harp.
Let them make music for Adonai
who delights in Adonai's people.

Adonai crowns humble ones with salvation.
Let the saints rejoice in honor,
Let them sing for joy on their beds.
Praises of God be in their mouths
and a two-edged sword in their hands.

Retribution on the nations
and punishment on the peoples
binding royalty in restraint
and nobility in rings of iron:
the judgment decreed for them,
such is the glory of the saints.

Hallelujah!

PSALM 150

Antiphon *Be merciful
as your Abba is merciful.*   Lk 6:36

Hallelujah!

To El in the sanctuary, give praise.
In the mighty heavens, give praise.
For the works of power, give praise.
For surpassing greatness, give praise.

With sounding of trumpet, give praise.
With harp and lyre, give praise.
With tambourine and dance, give praise.
With flute and string, give praise.

With cymbals clashing, give praise.
With cymbals resounding, give praise.
Let all that has breath praise Adonai!

Hallelujah!

• • •

The psalms are properly called
tehillim *(songs of praise) in Hebrew
and* psalmoi *(songs to be sung to the lyre)
in Greek; all the psalms have a musical quality.*
See *Introduction to the Liturgy of the Hours,* 103

a cosmology of the ancients

Canticles

*Think of a Canticle
as a Poem or a Song
that has been inserted into a text,
as if you were writing a letter
or recording a video for a loved one
and included in it their favorite poem or song.*

*They are provided here to use as you wish
(or not at all)
on the mornings and evenings of the days of the week
as they are used in the* Liturgy of the Hours.

*One way to pray them is to ponder
what kind of melody would be a good fit.*

1st - 7th & 15th - 21st

DANIEL 3:57-90

Antiphon *Taking the five loaves and the two fishes,
looking up to heaven, he blessed, and broke,
and gave them to the disciples
to set before the crowd.* Lk 9:16

Bless the Lord, all you works of the Lord,
exalt and sing praise to forever.
Angels of the Lord, bless the Lord,
You heavens, bless the Lord,
All you waters above the heavens, bless the Lord,
All you powers, bless the Lord,
Sun and moon, bless the Lord,
Stars of heaven, bless the Lord.

All you rain and dew, bless the Lord,
All you winds, bless the Lord,
Fire and heat, bless the Lord,
Ice and cold, bless the Lord,
Dews and falling snows, bless the Lord,
Snows and frosts, bless the Lord,
Nights and days, bless the Lord,
Light and darkness, bless the Lord,
Lightning and clouds, bless the Lord.

Let the earth bless the Lord,
exalt and sing praise to forever.
You mountains and hills, bless the Lord,
All things growing in the ground, bless the Lord,
Seas and rivers, bless the Lord,
Springs and rain, bless the Lord,
Sea monsters and swimmers, bless the Lord,
All you birds of the air, bless the Lord,
All you wild beasts and cattle, bless the Lord,
You sons and daughters, bless the Lord.

O Israel, bless the Lord,
exalt and sing praise to forever.
Priests of the Lord, bless the Lord,
Servants of the Lord, bless the Lord,
Spirits and souls of the just, bless the Lord,
You holy and humble in heart, bless the Lord,
Hananiah, Azariah, and Mishael, bless the Lord,
exalt and sing praise to forever...

Give thanks to the Lord, who is good,
whose mercy endures to forever.
Bless the God of "gods"
all you who worship the Lord;
sing praise and give thanks to the One God
whose mercy endures to forever.

•

SUNDAY MORNINGS

8th - 14th & 22nd - 30th

DANIEL 3:52-57

Antiphon *God sent the Son into the cosmos*
not to condemn, but that the cosmos
might be saved through him. Jn 3:17

Blessed are you, **O Lord**, God of our ancestors,
praiseworthy and exalted above all forever.

Blessed is your glorious and holy name,
praiseworthy and exalted above all forever.

Blessed are you in the temple of your sacred glory,
praiseworthy and exalted above all forever.

Blessed are you who sit high on the cherubim
and look into the depths,
praiseworthy and exalted above all forever.

Blessed are you on your royal throne,
praiseworthy and exalted above all forever.

Blessed are you in the dome of heaven,
to be hymned and glorified forever.

Bless the Lord, all you works of the Lord,
sing praise and high exaltation forever.

• • •

My book, sir philosopher, is the nature of created things,
and it is always at hand when I wish to read the words of God.
Anthony of Egypt, see *Praktikos* (#92) by Evagrius Ponticus

SUNDAY EVENINGS

1st - 30th

REVELATION 19:1b,2a,5b,6b,7

Antiphon   *We are an Easter people*
           *and **alleluia** is our song.*   St. Augustine

Alleluia!
Salvation and glory and power are to our God,
whose judgments are true and just.

Alleluia!
Praise our God, all you servants of the Lord,
you small and you great, who hold God in awe.

Alleluia!
The Lord is reigning, our God, the Almighty.
Let us rejoice and let us exult,
and we will give the glory to the Lord.

Alleluia!
The day has come
for the marriage of the Lamb,
and the bride has prepared herself.

• • •

The normal way we become best friends is by spending so much time with each other that we become happy to accomplish nothing but to waste time together. The best definition of prayer is wasting time with God, who is the good kind of jealous for this kind of time, and so Jesus says, 'I call you friend.'   See John 15

1st - 7th

ISAIAH 2:2-5

Antiphon   *Blessed are the peacemakers,*
for they will be called
sons and daughters of God.   Mt 5:9

In the last of the days
the mountain of Adonai's temple
will be established as chief of the mountains,
raised above the hills.

All the nations will stream to it.
Many peoples will come and say,
"Come, let us go up to the mountain of Adonai,
to the house of the God of Jacob,
who will teach us the ways
so we may walk in the path."

Indeed, from Zion the law will go out
and from Jerusalem the word of Adonai,
who will judge between the nations
and settle disputes for many peoples.

They will beat their swords into plowshares
and their spears into pruning hooks.
Nations will not take up the sword against nations,
and they will train for war no more.

House of Jacob, come!
Let us walk in Adonai's light.

●

MONDAY MORNINGS

8th - 14th

1 CHRONICLES 29:10b-13

Antiphon *Every thing we have to give
is from you, our God.*   1Chr 29:14b

Praise be to you, Adonai, God of Israel,
our Abba from everlasting to everlasting.

To you, Adonai, are the greatness and power
and glory and majesty and splendor
for all in the heavens and on the earth.

To you, Adonai, are the reign
and exaltation as head over all,
and wealth and honor from before you.

And you rule over all in your hand,
strength and power in your hand,
to lift up and give strength to all.

Now, our God, we give thanks to you
and praise your name and your glory.

•

---

*I want
not the things
you have, but you.*
Paul to the Corinthians 2 Cor 12:14

MONDAY MORNINGS
15th - 21st

SIRACH 36:1-6,13-22

Antiphon *The Lord hears the cry of the poor;*
blessed be the Lord. Ps 34

Come to our aid, God of all;
let all the nations be in fear of you.
Raise your hand to the foreign nations,
that they may see your might.

As you have used us to show them your holiness,
so now use them to show us your glory.
They will know as we know
that there is no God but you.

Give new signs and work new wonders;
show the splendor of your right hand and arm…

Gather all the tribes of Jacob,
that they may inherit the land as at the beginning.
Show mercy to the people called by your name:
Israel, whom you named your firstborn.

Have pity on your holy city, Jerusalem,
the foundation for your throne.
Fill Zion with your majesty,
and your temple with your glory.

Give witness of your deeds of old;
fulfill the prophecies spoken in your name.
Reward those who have hoped in you,
and let your prophets be proven true.

Hear the prayers of your servants,
as you are good to your people.
Thus all will know to the ends of the earth
that you are God eternal.

•

Perhaps
the basic sin in
the psalms is idolatry,
letting anything have priority
over God. Perhaps the clearest sign
that I am serving a lifeless idol is when
I am no longer able to hear the cry of the poor.

MONDAY MORNINGS
22nd - 30th

ISAIAH 42:10-16

Antiphon *I, your Lord,*
have called you for justice. Is 42:6a

Sing to Adonai a new song,
praise from the ends of the earth!

Ones going down to the sea and all in it,
and the islands, the ones living in them,
and the desert and its towns
and settlements where Kedar lives,
let them arise, let them sing for joy,

and the people of Sela
let them shout from the top of mountains.
Let them give to Adonai the glory
and proclaim praise in the islands.

Adonai will march out like the mighty human
and stir up zeal like a warrior,
and shouting and raising a cry
will triumph over enmity.

I was silent for a long time
and held back in quiet;
like a woman bearing a child,
I cry out and gasp and pant.

I will lay waste mountains and hills
letting all their vegetation dry up;
I will turn rivers into islands
and dry up pools.

I will lead blind ones by ways they did not know;
along paths they did not know I will guide them.
I will turn what is dark before them into light
and rough places into smooth.

These things I will do
and I will not forsake them.

• • •

God of mercy,
your Son ministered to all who came to him.
Give strength to your sons and daughters
who have lost their health and freedom
to the slavery of addiction.
Give them your grace in the work of recovery
and bring them to the freedom of sobriety.
To those who care for them,
grant wisdom to know when to help
and the patient love that perseveres.
Amen.

Prayer in an Addictive Culture
drawn from the *Book of Blessings*

MONDAY EVENINGS

1st - 30th

EPHESIANS 1:3-10

Antiphon   *Jesus called to himself the Twelve and began to send them out two by two.*   Mk 6:7a

Blessed be the God and Abba
of our Lord Jesus Christ,
who has blessed us in Christ
with every spiritual blessing in the heavens.

God chose us in Christ
before the foundation of the world,
to be holy and free of blemish before him.

In love, God gave us a destiny:
as parents adopt, through Jesus Christ himself,
in accord with the good pleasure of God's will
to the praise of the glory of grace
by which we are favored as God's beloved.

In Christ we have the redemption,
through his blood the forgiveness of sins
in accord with the riches of his grace
which he made abound to us.

In all wisdom and intelligence
the mystery of God's will is made known to us
in accord with God's good pleasure and purpose:

A stewardship of the fullness of time,
heading up all things in Christ,
the things in the heavens and the things on earth.

• • •

TUESDAY MORNINGS

1st - 7th

ISAIAH 26:1b-4,7-9,12

Antiphon *My soul yearns for you in the night;
within me my spirit longs for you.*

Our city is strong;
salvation makes walls and rampart.
Open gates, so the just nation may enter,
the one keeping faiths.

Your steadfast mind will keep peace,
peace because of trusting.
Trust in Adonai to forever,
for in Yah Adonai is the Rock of eternities…

The path of justice is level;
the Upright One smooths the way of the just.
Yes, in the way of your laws, Adonai, we wait,
for your name and your renown
are the desire of our heart.

My soul yearns for you in the night;
within me my spirit longs for you.
Just as your judgments are on the earth,
so people of the world learn justice…

Adonai, you establish for us peace;
indeed all we have accomplished
you did for us.

•

8th - 14th

TOBIT 13:1b-8

Antiphon *Behold,*
I make all things new. Rev 21:5b

Blessed be God who lives forever
and the reign of our God for all ages,
who scourges but then has mercy,
casts down to the deepest grave
and brings up from the great abyss.
No one can escape this hand.

Israelites, acknowledge before the nations
God who has scattered you among them
and even there shown you great mercy.

Let God be exalted by every living being
because our Lord is our God,
our Abba and God forever.

Though scourged for your iniquities,
mercy will be on you all;
you will be gathered from all the nations
among whom you have been scattered.

With all your heart and soul
turn with honesty to the Lord
who will turn the face to you
and no longer hide.

See now what has been done for you,
and with full voice praise Adonai.
Bless the Lord of justice
and exalt the Ruler of the ages.

In the land of my exile I acknowledge the Lord
and make known to a sinful nation
this power and majesty:
"Turn, you sinners, and do right before the Lord,
who may look upon you with favor and mercy."

My God, I will exalt you
and rejoice in the Ruler of Heaven.
Let all speak of this majesty
in Jerusalem with exaltation.

●

What the prophet
does is not so much predict
the future as to so accurately describe
the present that it becomes clear what is going
to happen unless we change our collective ways.

TUESDAY MORNINGS
15th - 21st

ISAIAH 38:10-14,17b-20

Antiphon   *The living alive praise Adonai.*

I asked, "Must I go in the prime of my days
through the gates of Sheol;
must I be robbed of the rest of my years?"

I said, "I will no longer see Adonai,
Adonai in the land of the living.
As a dweller of the place of cessation
I will look on humanity no longer."

My house was pulled down
and taken from me
like the tent of my shepherd;
I rolled up my life,
as a weaver cuts off from a loom.

From day to night you made an end of me.
I waited till dawn;
all my bones are broken as by a lion.
From day to night you made an end of me.

Like a swift or thrush I cried;
I moaned like the dove.
My eyes to the heavens grew weak.
Lord, troubles are at me; come to my aid…

In your love you have kept my self
out of the pit of destruction;
indeed you put behind your back all my sins.

Sheol cannot praise you
and death cannot sing to you praise,
nor can those going down the pit
hope for your faithfulness.

The living alive praise you, as I do this day.
Fathers and mothers tell the children
all about your faithfulness.

Adonai saves us;
we will play our stringed instruments
and sing in the temple of Adonai
all the days of our lives.

•

For the Christian,
Easter makes all the difference,
and Easter is not just about our earthly
death. By the time we get to heaven, we will have
let go of everything unhealed about us, mainly through
forgiving enemies, family, friends, ourselves, even God. Jesus
is inviting us to the extent made possible by grace to live right
now today as if all this has happened, to be fully alive right now.

22nd - 30th

DANIEL 3:26-27,29,34-41b

Antiphon   *Lord, do not withhold your mercy.*

Blessed be you, Lord, God of our ancestors,
your name worthy of praise and glory forever.

For you are just in all you do;
all your deeds are true and your ways upright,
and all your judgments are true…

We have sinned and broken your law
in turning from you;
in all ways possible we have sinned…

For the sake of your name,
do not give us up to forever
and do not void your covenant.

Do not take your mercy from us
for the sake of Abraham your beloved,
for the sake of Isaac your servant,
and Israel, your holy one,

to whom you promised to multiply
descendants like the stars of heaven
and like the sand on the shore of the sea.

For we, Lord, have become
least of the other nations
and are brought low in the world this day
because of our sins.

We have in our day no ruler, prophet, or leader,
no burnt offering, sacrifice, oblation or incense,
no place to make an offering before you
and so find your favor.

But with a contrite heart and a humble spirit
may we be accepted
as if they were burnt offerings of rams and bulls
or thousands of fat lambs.

As such may our sacrifice be seen by you today
and may we follow you without reserve,
for no shame will come to those who trust you.

And so we follow you with all our heart;
we fear you and seek your face.

• • •

Let nothing trouble.
Let nothing frighten.
Everything passes.
God never changes.
Patience obtains.
Whoever has God
wants for nothing.
God alone is enough.

Saint Teresa of Avila, d. 1582
written in the margin of her breviary

TUESDAY EVENINGS
1st - 30th

REVELATION 4:8b,11; 5:9,10,12,13b

Antiphon
Holy, Holy, Holy,
Lord God Almighty
who was and is and is to come.   Rev 4:8b

Worthy are you, our Lord and our God,
to receive the glory and honor and power,
for you have created all things,
and by your will all things were created and are.

Worthy are you to receive the scroll and unseal it
for you were sacrificed, and by your blood
ransomed for God those from every
tribe and tongue and people and nation.

You made of them for our God
a realm of royals and priests,
and thus will they reign over the earth.

Worthy is the Lamb, sacrificed to receive
the power and riches and wisdom and strength
and honor and glory and blessing.

• • •

Thomas Merton's friend Robert Lax: 'What you should say is that you want to be a saint... Don't you believe that God will make you what God created you to be, if you will consent to let God do it? All you have to do is desire it.'

See *The Seven Storey Mountain* by Thomas Merton

WEDNESDAY MORNINGS

1st - 7th

JUDITH 16:1,13-15

Antiphon   *O Lord, you are great and glorious,*
wonderful in strength, invincible.

Begin a song to my God with timbrels;
sing to my Lord with cymbals.
Sing to my Lord a new song;
exalt and acclaim the name.

I will sing to my God a new song;
O Lord, you are great and glorious,
wonderful in strength and unbeatable.

Let your every creature serve you,
for you spoke, and they were made.
You sent forth your spirit,
and they were created;
no one can resist your word.

Mountain foundations are shaken by waters
and rocks melt like wax at your glance.
But to those who fear you, you show mercy.

•

To sing is
to pray twice.
Saint Augustine

1 SAMUEL 2:1-10

Antiphon *My spirit rejoices in God my Savior.* Lk 1:47

My heart rejoices in Adonai,
my horn is lifted high in Adonai.

My mouth boasts over enmity,
for I delight in being delivered.
There is no Holy One like Adonai,
indeed there is no one who compares;
there is no Rock like our God.

Arrogant pride is coming from their mouth.
Do not keep talking so proudly
or proudly let arrogance come from your mouth,
for Adonai is God who knows,
by whom all deeds are weighed.

Bows of warriors are broken
but those stumbling are armed with strength.
The full hire themselves out for more food,
but the hungry ones hunger no more.
She who was barren bore seven sons;
blessed with many, another is pining away.

Adonai allows death and is making alive,
brings down to Sheol and is raising up.
Adonai allows poverty and is sending wealth,
humbling and exalting,
raising the poor from the dust
and the needy from ash-heaps
to sit with royals and inherit thrones of honor.

For Adonai's are the foundations of the earth,
setting the world upon them.
The feet of the saints will be guarded
but doers of the bad will be silenced in darkness.

For not by strength does the human prevail;
Adonai shatters opposition,
thundering from the heavens.
Adonai will judge the ends of the earth,
give strength, and raise the horn
of the one chosen and anointed.

•

*All shall be well
and all shall be well and
all manner of things shall be well.*
Julian of Norwich, d. 1416

WEDNESDAY MORNINGS
15th - 21st

ISAIAH 61:10-62:5

Antiphon *My God has clothed me*
in garments of salvation.

To delight, I delight in Adonai,
my soul rejoices in my God,
who clothed me in garments of salvation
and arrayed me in a robe of justice,
as spouses dress their heads like priests
and adorn themselves with jewels,

for as the soil makes the sprout come up
and as a garden makes seeds to grow
so will Sovereign Adonai
make justice spring up
and praise before all the nations.

For the sake of Zion, I will not keep silent;
for the sake of Jerusalem I will not remain quiet,
till vindication comes out like the dawn
and salvation blazes like a torch.

The nations will see your vindication
and all the rulers your glory
and you will be called by a new name
that the mouth of Adonai will bestow.
You will be a crown of splendor
in the hand of Adonai
and a royal diadem in the hand of your God.

No longer will you be called One Being Deserted,
nor will your name be called Desolation,
but you will be called "my delight is in her"
and your land "espoused."
Adonai will delight in you
and your land will be married.

As young folks marry each other,
your Builder will marry you;
and as a newlywed rejoices over a spouse,
so will your God rejoice over you.

•

Intimacy is a basic human need and
I tend to it or it will find unhealthy ways
to tend to me. It is the grace of being known,
the blessing of being with a friend or a spouse who
knows me so well that I am free to simply be who I am.

See *Being Spouses* by Stephen Joseph Wolf

WEDNESDAY MORNINGS
22nd - 30th

ISAIAH 33:13-16

Antiphon *Blessed is the one who works justice*
and speaks honesty.

Hear what I have done, you who are far away!
And acknowledge my power, you who are near.

Sinners are terrified in Zion
and trembling grips the godless.
Who of us can dwell in fire that consumes?
Who of us can dwell in everlasting burning?

One working justice and speaking honesty,
rejecting the gains of extortion,
waving off acceptance of the bribe,
stopping ears from hearing of bloodshed,
shutting eyes to not gaze on the bad:

That one will dwell on the heights
in a mountain fortress refuge,
supplied with bread and waters never-failing.

• • •

If you can figure out its name, it may be helpful to then
choose a daily church bell or alarm ringtone to remind you
to simply remember once a day what your personal vocation is.

See *Discovering Your Personal Vocation* by Herbert Alphonso, Jesuit
(If this helps to ponder it, I think mine is *holy honesty*. – SJW)

WEDNESDAY EVENINGS

1st - 30th

COLOSSIANS 1:12-20

Antiphon *Who follows me will have the light of life.* Jn 8:12c

Give joyful thanks to the Abba who made you fit
for your part of the lot of the saints in light,

who delivered us out of the authority of darkness,
transitioning us into the realm of the beloved Son
in whom we have redemption,
the forgiveness of our sins.

The Son is the image of the invisible God,
the firstborn of all creation.
In him all things were created,
in the heavens and on the earth,
the visible and the invisible,
whether thrones, lordships, rulers or authorities.

All creation has come to be through and for him.
He is before all things,
and in him all things hold together.

He is the head of the body, the church,
and the beginning, the firstborn from the dead,
so that in all things he may hold the first place.

In him all the fullness was well pleased to dwell,
and through him reconciliation to himself
of all things on earth and things in the heavens,
making peace through the blood of his cross.

• • •

THURSDAY MORNINGS

THURSDAY MORNINGS

1st - 7th

JEREMIAH 31:10-14

Antiphon *They will be my people and I will be their God*
for they will return to me with all their heart.

Jer 24:7b

Hear, nations, the word of Adonai;
proclaim it to distant coastlands and say:
"The One who scattered Israel
will gather them and watch them
as one who is shepherd to a flock."

For Adonai will ransom and redeem Jacob
from the hand of those with more strength.

They will come and they will shout
up on the height of Zion
and they will rejoice in the bounty of Adonai,
the grain and new wine and oil,
and younglings of the flock and herd;
and they themselves like a well-watered garden
will sorrow no more, not again.

Then the maiden will be glad in dance,
and young men together with the old.
I will turn their mourning into gladness;
I will comfort them, replacing sorrow with joy.
I will satisfy with abundance the self of the priests
and my people will be filled with my bounty,
declares Adonai.

•

THURSDAY MORNINGS
8th - 14th

ISAIAH 40:10-17

Antiphon   *A voice of one cried out in the desert:*
prepare the way of the Lord.   Mk 1:3

See! Sovereign Adonai comes with power,
and with a ruling arm.
See! And with reward
accompanied with recompense.

Like a shepherd tending the flock
and gathering lambs in the arms,
carrying them in the heart
and leading gently those with young.

Who can measure the waters in a hand's hollow?
or mark off the heavens with handbreadths?
or hold the dust of the earth in a basket?
or weigh mountains on a scale
or hills in a balance?

Who has understood the mind of Adonai?
What human has given counsel or instruction,
or whom was consulted for enlightenment
and teaching about what is right
and teaching knowledge?
Who can show the path of understanding?

Surely nations are like drops in a bucket
and are regarded as dust on a scale.
Surely islands are weighed like fine dust.

Even Lebanon is not sufficient to make fire,
nor their animals sufficient for burnt-offering.
Before God, all the nations are as nothing,
regarded as worthless and less than nothing.

•

God questions:
*Where were you when
I founded the earth? Have
you in your days ordered morning
and shown the dawn its place? How
is the lightning sent and the east wind
scattered over the earth? Who has wisdom
to count the clouds? Do you know the time
of birth of a mountain goat? Do you give strength
to the horse? Does the eagle soar at your command?*
And Job answers: *Surely I have spoken without under-
standing of things more wonderful than me I cannot know.
I retract my words and repent in dust and ash.* See Job 38-42

THURSDAY MORNINGS
15th - 21st

ISAIAH 12:1b-6

Antiphon   *The crowds asked John the Baptist,*
           what then shall we do?   Lk 3:10

I will praise you, Adonai.
Though you were angry with me,
your anger turned away and you comforted me.

Surely God is my salvation!
I will trust and will not be afraid
for Yah is my strength and my song.

Adonai became for me salvation
and you will draw with joy
waters from wells of salvation…

Give thanks to Adonai! Call on the name!
Make the deeds known among the nations!
Proclaim that the name is exalted!

Sing to Adonai, who has done glory!
Let this be known to all the world.

Shout! And sing for joy, dwellers of Zion!
For great in your midst is the Holy One of Israel.

•

Crowds, share your food and second coat with those in need.
Tax collectors, collect no more than what you know you ought.
Soldiers, do not extort anyone, and be satisfied with you wages.

THURSDAY MORNINGS

22nd - 30th

ISAIAH 66:7-14a

Antiphon   *Know this:*
           the reign of God is at hand.   Lk 10:11b

"**Before she goes into labor** she gives birth;
before pain comes upon her, she delivers a son.
Who has heard of such as this?
Who has seen such as these?

Can a country be born in one day
or a nation be brought forth in one moment?
Yet she is in labor,
then Zion gives birth to her children.

Do I bring to the moment of birth
and not give delivery?"
asks your God Adonai;
"Do I bring one to delivery and then close up?

Rejoice with Jerusalem and be glad for her!
All who love her, rejoice with her!
Rejoice, all who mourn over her,

for you will nurse and you will be satisfied
at the breast of her comforts,
for you will drink deeply and you will delight
in the overflow of her abundance."

Isaiah 66, continued

For this says Adonai:
"See, I extend peace to her like a river,
and wealth of nations like a flooding stream,
and you will nurse, being carried at her side,
and you will be playdanced on her knees.

As a child is comforted by a mother,
so will I comfort you
and over Jerusalem you will be comforted.

When you see, your heart will rejoice
and your bones will flourish like the grass."

• • •

Lord, to those who have hunger, give bread;
and to those who have bread,
give hunger for justice.

A Latin American Prayer

THURSDAY EVENINGS

1st - 30th

REVELATION 11:17-18, 12:10-12a

Antiphon   *I am the Alpha and the Omega, says the Lord God, the one who is and who was and who is to come, the Almighty.*   Rev 1:8

We thank you, Lord God Almighty,
the One who is and who was;
you have taken your great power and reign.

The nations raged and your anger came,
and the time to judge the dead
and to reward your servants and prophets,
the saints, and those fearing your name,
the small and the great…

Now have come the salvation and power
and reign of our God and the authority of Christ.
The accuser of our brothers and sisters was cast,
accusing them before our God day and night.

Their victory was because of the blood of the Lamb
and by the word of their witness.
They loved their life into their death,
and so be glad, you heavens,
and all you dwelling in them.

• • •

FRIDAY MORNINGS

1st - 7th

ISAIAH 45:15-25

Antiphon *The reign of God
is justice and peace
and joy in the Holy Spirit.* Rom 14:17

Truly, **God**, you hide yourself,
Saving God of Israel.
Makers of idols will know shame and disgrace,
all going off together in disgrace.

Israel will be saved by Adonai,
salvation everlasting.
You will not know shame or disgrace to the ages.

For this says Adonai, creating the heavens,
who fashioned and made and formed the earth,
creating it to be not an empty waste,
but formed to be inhabited,

"I am Adonai, and there is no other.
Not in secret did I speak,
from some place in a dark land,
saying to descendants of Jacob, 'seek me in vain.'
I, Adonai, speak truth and delare right things.

Gather together and come!
Assemble together, fugitives of the nations.
Those who carry idols of wood do not know:
they are praying to no-gods that cannot save.

Declare and present! Let them counsel together!
Who foretold this from long ago?
Who declared this from the distant past?
Not I, Adonai? There is no god apart from me,
God just and Saving; there is none but me.

Turn to me and be saved,
all you ends of the earth,
for I am God and there is no other.

By myself I swore integrity out of my mouth,
the word that will not be revoked.

Indeed, in front of me every knee will bow,
and every tongue will swear, and say,
'In Adonai alone are justice and strength,'

to whom will come and be shamed
all who have raged otherwise."
In Adonai they will be found just
and all the descendants of Israel will exult.

•

---

*If someone is gay
and searches for the Lord
and has good will, who am I to judge?*
Pope Francis, July 29, 2013

FRIDAY MORNINGS
8th - 14th

JEREMIAH 14:17b-22

Antiphon *Before I formed you in the womb*
I knew you.

Jer 1:5

> *On sin,*
> *a pondering:*
> *Lord, when I examine*
> *my conscience, every day*
> *I am aware of sin, and it seems*
> *always to be that in that moment of*
> *sinning I was not aware of your love for*
> *me. Why do I forget that you love me? How*
> *can I stay aware of your love? Is it even possible?*

A Consciousness Examen in Three Minutes (an aware prayer)

1st – *Replay your day. Pick out a high point in it – a good thing you did, like going out of your way to help someone… Give God thanks for the opportunity.*

2nd – *Replay your day again. This time pick out a low point – a bad thing you did, like putting down someone who really needs to be lifted up… Ask Jesus for forgiveness.*

3rd – *Look ahead to tomorrow to a critical point – a hard thing you must do, like dealing with a personal problem… Ask the Holy Spirit for help with it.*

See *Challenge 2000: A Daily Meditation Program based on the Spiritual Exercises of Saint Ignatius* by Mark Link, Jesuit

Let my eyes overflow with tears
by night, by day, without cease,
for the grievous wounds suffered
by the virgin daughter of my people,
a very crushing blow.

If I go out in the country, see: ones slain by sword!
If I go in the city, see: the ravages of famine!
Indeed, both prophet and priest
have gone to a land they do not know.

To reject you rejected Judah?
Is Zion despised by your self?
Why have you afflicted us so we have no healing?

Our hope is for peace, but no good happens;
for a time of healing, but see: the terror!
We are aware, Adonai, of our no-good ways
and the guilt of our ancestors;
indeed we ourselves sin against you.

For the sake of your Name, neither despise us
nor dishonor the throne of your glory.
Remember, and break not your covenant with us!

Is there one among the worthless nations
that can bring rain or send showers from the skies?
Is that One not you, our God Adonai?
And so we hope in you, for you do all these things.

•

FRIDAY MORNINGS
15th - 21st

HABAKKUK 3:2-4,13a,15-19

Antiphon *Looking round on them with anger,
Jesus grieved at their hardness of heart.*   Mk 3:5

Adonai, I heard your fame;
I stand in awe of your deeds, Adonai.
Now, in the midst of years, renew them!
In the midst of years, make them known!
Even in wrath you remember mercy.

Eloah came from Teman,
the Holy One from the Mount of Paran.
The heavens are covered with glory
and the earth is filled with praise

like the splendor of the rays of the sunrise
or the hand from a hiding place of power…
You came out to deliver your people,
to deliver your anointed one…

You trample on the sea,
your horses churning up the great waters.
My heart heard and she trembled,
at the sound my lips quivered;

decay crept into my bones
and my legs trembled.
Yet, I will wait patiently for the day,
calamity to come on the nation invading.

Though the fig tree does not bud
and there is no grape on the vine,
the crops of the olive fail
and fields produce no food,

the sheep cut themselves off from the pen
and there are no cattle in the stalls,
yet will I rejoice in Adonai
and be joyful in the God of my salvation.

Sovereign Adonai, my strength,
makes my feet like that of the deer,
makes me go to the heights.

•

Lord my God, it
has happened again
and anger is visiting me.
I still hear your gospel call to
love enemies, to pray for persecutors,
and to forgive. Trusting in your way I pray:
I am still angry with N. Judging is your job alone
for you alone have all the data. Like me, N. is created in
your image and loved by you without limit. But there seems to be
something unhealed in N.; I know not what it is, and N. may not know
either, but you, Lord, you know: and I believe that you want to heal it.
This I ask you to do. Lay onto N. your healing touch.

See *Anger the Jesus Way* (reflections on Mark 3:1-6, the only time
the gospels specify the word *anger* for Jesus) by Stephen Joseph Wolf

FRIDAY MORNINGS
22nd - 30th

TOBIT 13:8-11,13-15

Antiphon *One of the seven angels showed me*
the holy city of Jerusalem
shining with the glory of God. Rev 21:10,11

Acknowledge the Lord in Jerusalem.

You Jerusalem, Holy City, will be scourged
for what your children have done.
The Lord will again have mercy
on the children of the just.

Acknowledge the Lord as is deserving
and bless the Ruler of the ages,
that your sanctuary will be built in you again
with joy and cheer by all who were exiles,
and love for all generations
those who were distressed.

A bright light will shine
to all the ends of the earth;
many nations will come from far away.

Those living in the most remote parts of earth
will come to your holy Name,
bearing in their hands
gifts for the Ruler of Heaven.

Generation to generation will give joyful praise
and the name of the Lord will be great forever…

Then, children of the just, rejoice and exult;
be gathered together
and bless the Lord of the ages.

Happy are those who love you,
and happy will be those
who rejoice in prosperity.

Happy also are all
who grieve over your afflictions
for they will rejoice with you
and give witness to your joy forever.

My soul, praise the Lord,
the mega Ruler.

• • •

Come, Holy Spirit,
fill the hearts of your faithful;
set fire in us your confirming love.
Give us wisdom to seek the face of God,
understanding of our baptism in Christ, and
right judgment to discern his call in freedom.
Give us courage to say yes to our vocations,
knowledge of what Jesus teaches,
and reverence for the ways of the Abba.
Give us wonder and awe in your presence,
that the witness we give to the resurrection of the Son
may be pleasing to the Abba
and help you, Holy Spirit, renew the face of the earth.

Easter Prayer of the Confirmed

FRIDAY EVENINGS
1st - 30th

REVELATION 15:3b-4

Antiphon   *They sang the song of Moses,*
the servant of God,
and the song of the Lamb.   Rev 15:3a

Great and wonderful are your works,
Lord God Almighty.
Just and true are your ways,
Ruler of the nations.

Who will not fear, O Lord,
or glorify your name?

Only you are holy.
All the nations will come
and worship before you;
your ordinances are shown to all.

• • •

Behold God
beholding you
…and smiling.
Anthony de Mello, Jesuit

SATURDAY MORNINGS

1st - 7th

EZEKIEL 36:24-28

Antiphon *Let any who thirst
come to me and drink.*   Jn 7:37

I will take you out of the nations
and I will gather you from all the countries,
and I will bring you back into your land.

I will sprinkle on you clean waters,
and you will be clean from all your impurities,
and from all your idols I will cleanse you.

I will give you a new heart
and I will put inside you a new spirit,
and I will remove the stone-heart from your flesh
and I will give you a flesh-heart,

and I will put inside you my Spirit
and I will move you to follow in my decrees
and my laws you will be careful to keep,

and you will live in the land I gave your ancestors,
and you will be my people
and I will be your God.

•

All repressed emotions are stored in the body...
The deep rest of contemplative prayer reduces the
defenses that hold these oppressive feelings in the unconscious.
See *Divine Therapy & Addiction* by Thomas Keating, Trappist monk

SATURDAY MORNINGS
8th - 14th

EXODUS 15:1b-4,8-13,17-18

Antiphon   *By faith they passed*
            through the Red Sea
            as if it were dry land.   Heb 11:29a

I will sing to Adonai, exalting exaltation,
who hurled horse and rider into the sea.

My strength and my song,
Yah has become to me salvation.
I will praise my God
and exalt the God of my ancestors.

Adonai the warrior, named Adonai,
hurled Pharaoh's army of chariots into the sea…
By the blast of your nostrils the waters piled up;
like a wall they stood firm in the heart of the sea,
raging deep waters congealed.

The enemy boasted, "I will pursue and overtake,
divide the spoils and gorge on them myself;
I will draw my sword;
my hand will destroy them."

You blew with your breath
and the sea covered them;
they sank like lead in the mighty waters.

Who is like you among "gods," Adonai?
Who like you is majestic and holy,
awesome in glory and working wonders?
You stretched your right hand
and the earth swallowed them.

You will lead in your love
the people you redeemed.
You will guide them in strength
to your holy dwelling…

You will bring them in and you will plant them
on the mountain of your inheritance,
the dwelling place you made, Adonai,
the sanctuary, Lord, that your hands established.
Adonai will reign forever and ever.

•

Big Stories of
Hebrew Scripture:
1 Creation
2 The Great Flood
3 Covenant with Abraham
4 Exodus out of Slavery in Egypt
5 Desert Wandering & the Promised Land
6 Judges, Prophets, Royals & Temple Priesthood
7 The Babylonian Exile & then Return from the Exile

SATURDAY MORNINGS
15th - 21st

WISDOM 9:1-6,9-11

Antiphon *And Jesus advanced
in wisdom and age and favor
before God and humans.* Lk 2:52

God of my ancestors, Lord of mercy,
who made all things by your word
and through your wisdom framed humanity
to be master of the creatures you have created,
and to govern the world in holiness and justice
and judge justly and with an upright heart,

give me Wisdom, your companion at your throne,
and do not reject me from among your children,
for I am your servant, born of your handmaid,
a feeble human with a short life
and a weak understanding of justice and laws.

Though a human be
ever so perfect in human eyes,
without your Wisdom that same one
will be of no account…

With you is Wisdom,* who knows your works
and was present when you created the world,
who knows what is pleasing in your eyes
and what is right in accord with your ordinances.

* *Sophia, Lady Wisdom*

SATURDAY MORNINGS

Send her forth from the holy heavens
and dispatch her from your majestic throne,
that she may labor beside me
and I may learn what pleases you.

For she knows and understands all things
and will guide me to prudence in my actions
and guard me in her magnificence.

•

Sometime when you are in the presence of
what Thomas Merton called 'children in a moment
when they are really children,' ponder that there was a day
when God was exactly that tall and weighed exactly that much.

SATURDAY MORNINGS
22nd - 30th

DEUTERONOMY 32:1-12

Antiphon   *Praise the greatness of our God.*

Listen, **heavens**, and I will speak:
Hear, earth, the words of my mouth.
Let my teaching fall like the rain,
let my word descend like the dew,
like showers on grass,
like abundant rains on plants.

The name of Adonai I will proclaim,
and praise the greatness of our God.
The work of the Rock is perfect indeed;
all the ways of our faithful God are just
and without wrong, upright and just.

The children acted corruptly with no shame,
a generation warped and crooked.
Foolish and unwise people,
you repay Adonai in this way?
Did not your Abba create you
and make you and form you?

Remember the days of old!
Consider the years of generation and generation!
Ask your parents and they will tell you!
Ask your elders and they will explain to you

how the Most High gave inheritance to nations,
dividing sons and daughters of humanity
and setting up boundaries of peoples
by numbers of sons and daughters of Israel.

For the portion of Adonai is the people,
Jacob the allotment of inheritance,
found in desert land,
a barren and howling waste,
shielded with care,
guarded as the apple of the eye,

like an eagle stirring up the nest
and hovering over the young ones,
spreading wings to catch them
and carrying them on its flight feathers.

Led by Adonai alone,
no foreign "god" was with them.

• • •

---

*Is God the greatest? To speak of
God with a superlative such as Most
Powerful or Most Beautiful or the Greatest
would be to see God as merely the best within
created categories, but God is beyond categories of
creation, and so better language may be to refer to God
as Greatness-Itself or Power-Itself or Beauty-Itself, though
this remains imperfect. And yet we cannot not talk about God.*

SATURDAY EVENINGS

1st - 30th

PHILIPPIANS 2:6-11

Antiphon *Do nothing out of selfishness*
or for vainglory,
but humbly deem others
as greater than yourselves.   Phil 2:3

Christ Jesus, subsisting in the form of God,
did not deem equality with God
something to grab,
but emptied himself,
taking the form of a slave,
becoming in human likeness.

And being found in human fashion,
he humbled himself,
becoming obedient until death,
and death on a cross.

And so God highly exalted him,
and gave to him the name above every name,
that in the name of Jesus
every knee should bend,
of heavenly beings and earthly beings,
and beings under the earth;

And every tongue acknowledge
to the glory of God the Abba
that Jesus Christ is Lord.

• • •

AN INTRODUCTION TO PRAYER

Keep it **simple**.

Make the **time**, 20-60 minutes, or even 5.

Find a regular **place** and close the door;
a straight back **chair** is best.

Choose one **passage**;
trust that you have chosen the right one.

Take off the **shoes** and sit up.

Offer up your still incomplete
awareness of **illusions**.

Ask God to speak God's name
in the center of your being.

Take in a deep **breath**, hold, release.

Read the passage slowly;
when caught by a **word**, stop.

Breathe the word until it feels done,
as might a piece of gum.

When the mind **wanders** (it will),
breathe the word to come back.

If it is a **story**, be one of the characters and notice
what you see, hear, smell, taste and touch.

It is okay to not finish the passage, but if you do,
read it again and **choose** a word, phrase or image
for the rest of this prayer-time.

When time is up, give **thanks**.

MORE PASSAGES FOR PRAYER

The passages listed on these seven pages are in your Bible and in *A Jesus Breviary*

31 days of GOD's LOVE-CALL

1	Psalm 63:1-8
2	Psalm 46
3	Isaiah 55:1-13
4	Wisdom of Solomon 9:1-6,9-11
5	Psalm 23
6	Psalm 139:1-18,23-24
7	Isaiah 43:1-5a
8	Exodus 16:4-5,9,10b
9	Hosea 2:10-22
10	Psalm 131
11	Psalm 8
12	Psalm 103
13	Psalm 104
14	Psalm 19
15	1st Kings 19:4-9a,11-13
16	Jeremiah 29:11-14
17	Ezekiel 16:4-13
18	Jeremiah 18:1-6
19	Genesis 2:4-25
20	Genesis 1:24-31
21	Isaiah 54:4-10
22	Deuteronomy 30:15-20
23	Isaiah 62:1-5
24	Ecclesiastes 3:1-11,14b
25	Psalm 62:2-10,12,13a
26	Wisdom of Solomon 11:21-12:1
27	Psalm 91:1-12,14-16
28	Ezekiel 36:24-28
29	Ezekiel 37:1-14
30	Isaiah 40:1-11
31	Psalm 130

31 days of JESUS INCARNATE

#	Title	Reference
1	ANNUNCIATION	Luke 1:26-38
2	NATIVITY	Luke 2:15-21
3	THE MAJI	Matthew 2:1-12
4	SIMEON & ANNA	Luke 2:22-40
5	RETURN from EXILE	Matthew 2:19-23
6	TWELVE YEARS OLD	Luke 2:41-52
7	THE WORD	Prologue of the Gospel of John 1:1-14
8	BAPTISM	Matthew 3:13-17 Mk 1:9-11 Lk 3:21-22
9	TEMPTATION	Matt 4:1-11 Mark 1:12-13 Luke 4:1-13
10	REJECTION	Luke 4:14-30 Mt 13:54-58 Mk 6:1-6
11	SIMON, ANDREW...	Mark 1:14-20 Mt 4:12-22 Lk 5:1-11
12	DAY in the MINISTRY	Mk 1:29-39 Mt 4:23-25 Lk 4:38-44
13	NICODEMUS at NIGHT	John 3:1-21
14	WOMAN at the WELL	John 4:5-42
15	LEVI is CALLED	Mark 2:13-17 Luke 5:27-32

In Matthew 9:9-13 the tax-collector's name is Matthew.

#	Title	Reference
16	FIELD of GRAIN	Mark 2:23-28 Mt 12:1-8 Lk 6:1-5
17	THE TWELVE & THE WOMEN	Luke 6:12-19 & 8:1-3
		Matthew 10:1-4 Mark 3:13-19
18	LOVE YOUR ENEMIES	Matthew 5:43-48 Luke 6:27-36
19	THE FAMILY	Mark 3:20-21 John 10:20
		Mark 3:31-35 Matthew 12:46-50 Luke 8:19-21
20	THE BREAD of LIFE	John 6:52-53,60-69
21	DISCIPLES of the BAPTIZER	Luke 7:18-23 Mt 11:2-6
22	ANOINTING by a WOMAN	Luke 7:36-50
23	PROFESSION	Matt 16:13-20 Mk 8:27-33 Lk 9:18-21
24	TRANSFIGURATION	Mk 9:2-10 Mt 17:1-9 Lk 9:28-36
25	WOMAN CAUGHT in ADULTERY	John 8:2-11
26	RICH YOUNG MAN	Mt 19:16-22 Mk 10:17-27 Lk 18:18-30
27	JAMES & JOHN	Mark 10:35-45 Matthew 20:20-28
28	ZACCHAEUS	Luke 19:1-10
29	ENTRY on a DONKEY	Mark 11:1-10
		Matthew 21:1-11; Luke 19:28-40; John 12:12-19
30	CLEANSING the TEMPLE	Mark 11:15b-18
		Matthew 21:12-16 Luke 19:45-48 John 2:13-25
31	AUTHORITY QUESTIONED	
	Mark 11:27-33 Matthew 21:23-27 Luke 20:1-8	
	Mark 12:28-34 Matthew 22:34-40	

31 days of JESUS MIRACLES

1. WATER & WINE (1st of 6 or 7 Signs in John) John 2:1-11
2. CATCH of FISH   Luke 5:3-11
3. SON of a ROYAL OFFICIAL   John 4:46-54
4. DEMONIAC   Mark 1:21-28   Luke 4:31-37
5. LEPER   Matthew 8:1-4   Mark 1:40-45   Luke 5:12-16
6. PARALYTIC   Mark 2:1-12   Matthew 9:1-8   Luke 5:17-26
7. SICK MAN at BETHESDA   John 5:1-17
8. MAN with a WITHERED HAND   Mark 3:1-6
   Matthew 12:9-14   Luke 6:6-11
9. SERVANT of a CENTURIAN   Matt 8:5-13   Luke 7:1-10
10. SON of a WIDOW   Luke 7:11-17
11. CALMING of a STORM   Matthew 8:23-27
    Mark 4:35-41   Luke 8:22-25
12. GERASENE-GADARENE DEMONIAC   Mark 5:1-20
    Matthew 8:28-34   Luke 8:26-39
13. DAUGHTER of JAIRUS & WOMAN in the CROWD
    Luke 8:40-56   Matthew 9:18-26   Mark 5:21-43
14. TWO BLIND MEN   Mathew 9:27-31
15. POSSESSED MUTE   Matthew 9:32-35
16. FEEDING of FIVE THOUSAND   John 6:1-15
    Matthew 14:13-21   Mark 6:34-44   Luke 9:10-17
17. WALKING on WATER   John 6:16-21
    Mark 6:45-52   Matthew 14:22-33
18. WOMAN of CANAAN   Matthew 15:21-28   Mk 7:24-30
19. DEAF MUTE   Mark 7:31-37
20. FEEDING of FOUR THOUSAND   Mt 15:32-39   Mk 8:1-10
21. BLIND MAN of BETHSAIDA   Mark 8:22-26
22. POSSESSED BOY   Lk 9:37-43a   Mt 17:14-20   Mk 9:14-29
23. PROVISION for TEMPLE TAX   Matthew 17:22-27
24. MAN BORN BLIND   John 9:1-41
25. WOMAN CRIPPLED   Luke 13:10-17
26. MAN with DROPSY   Luke 14:1-6
27. TEN LEPERS   Luke 17:11-19
28. BLIND BARTIMAEUS   Mark 10:46-52
    Matthew 20:29-34   Luke 18:35-43
29. RAISING of LAZARUS   John 11:1-45
30. CURSING of a FIG TREE   Mark 11:12-14,20-25   Mt 21:18-22
31. HEALING of an EAR   Luke 22:47-51

31 days of JESUS PARABLES

1. NEW WINE — Mark 2:18-22   Mt 9:16-17   Lk 5:33-39
2. CHILDREN of the MARKETPLACE   Mt 11:12-19 Lk 7:28-35
3. THE SOWER & GOOD EARTH — Mark 4:3-20
   Matthew 13:3-23   Luke 8:4-15
4. GOOD SAMARITAN — Luke 10:29-37
5. RICH FOOL — Luke 12:16-21
6. RAVENS & LILIES — Luke 12:22-32   Matthew 6:25-34
7. GRAIN GROWING — Mark 4:26-29
8. MUSTARD SEED — Mark 4:30-32   Mt 13:31-32   Lk 13:18-19
   LEAVEN — Luke 13:20-21   Matthew 13:33
9. WEEDS & WHEAT — Matthew 13:24-30
10. TREASURE & PEARL & NET & HEAD of HOUSEHOLD
    Matthew 13:44-52
11. LATRINE — Mark 7:14-23   Mathew 15:10-20
12. VIGILANT SERVANT — Mark 13:32-37   Luke 12:35-40
13. FAITHFUL SERVANT — Matthew 24:45-51   Luke 12:42-48
14. BARREN FIG TREE — Luke 13:6-9
15. MEGA BANQUET — Luke 14:16-24   Mathew 22:1-14
16. FAMILY & TOWER & TROOPS & SALT — Luke 14:26-35
    Matthew 5:13, 10:37, 16:24   Mark 8:34-37, 9:49-50
17. ONE LOST SHEEP — Luke 15:1-7   Matthew 18:12-14
    ONE LOST COIN — Luke 15:8-10
18. LOST SON — Luke 15:11-32
19. STEWARD of INJUSTICE — Luke 16:1-13
20. RICH MAN & LAZARUS — Luke 16:19-31
21. UNFORGIVING DEBTOR — Matthew 18:21-35
22. UNPROFITABLE SERVANTS — Luke 17:7-10
23. PERSISTENT WIDOW — Luke 18:1-8
24. WORKERS in the VINEYARD — Matthew 20:1-16
25. PHARISEE & TAX COLLECTOR — Luke 18:9-14
26. TWO SONS — Matthew 21:28-32
27. TENANT FARMERS — Mark 12:1-11
    Matthew 21:33-46   Luke 20:9-19
28. TEN VIRGINS — Matthew 25:1-13
29. TALENTS — Matthew 25:14-30
    Luke 19:11-27 (mina coins)
30. SHEEP & GOATS & WORKS of MERCY — Matthew 25:31-46
31. VINE & BRANCHES — John 15:1-8

31 days of the PASCHAL MYSTERY of JESUS

1. MANY OTHER THINGS — John 20:30-31 & 21:25
2. ANOINTING at BETHANY — Mark 14:3-9 Matt 26:6-13
3. THE LAST SUPPER — Mark 14:22-26 Mt 26:26-30 Lk 22:14-20
4. FOOT WASHING — John 13:1-17
5. LAST SUPPER DISCOURSE — John 13:31-14:12 Lk 22:24-30
6. AGONY in the GARDEN — Mk 14:32f Mt 26:33f Lk 22:39f
7. BETRAYAL & ARREST — Luke 22:47-53
   Matthew 26:47-56 Mark 14:43-52 John 18:1-11
8. SANHEDRIN — Mk 14:53-64 Mt 26:57-68 Lk 22:54 Jn 18:12-14
9. PETER'S DENIAL — Luke 22:55-62
   Matthew 26:69-75 Mark 14:66-72 John 18:15-18,25-27
10. DEATH of JUDAS — Matthew 27:3-10 Acts 1:16-20
11. PILATE'S QUESTIONS — Luke 23:1-5
    Matthew 27:11-14 Mark 15:2-5 John 18:33-38a; 19:7-11
12. MOCKERY — Luke 22:63-65 & 23:6-12
    John 18:38-19:6 Mark 15:16-20 Matthew 27:27-31a
13. SENTENCE of DEATH — John 19:7-11a,12-16a
    Matthew 27:15-26 Mark 15:6-15 Luke 23:13-25
14. WAY of the CROSS — Lk 23:26-32 Mt 27:31f Mk 15:21 Jn 19:16bf
15. CRUCIFIXION — John 19:19-27
    Matthew 27:33-44 Mark 15:22-32 Luke 23:33-43
16. DEATH of JESUS — Mark 15:33f Mt 27:49f Lk 23:44f Jn 19:28f
17. BURIAL & GUARD — Mt 27:57f Mk 15:42f Lk 23:50f Jn 19:38f
18. THE EMPTY TOMB — Mark 16:1-8
19. THE EMPTY TOMB — Luke 24:1-12
20. THE EMPTY TOMB — John 20:1-10
21. THE EMPTY TOMB — Matthew 28:1-10
22. APPEARANCE to MARY of MAGDALA — John 20:11-18
    Mark 16:9-11
23. On the ROAD to EMMAUS — Luke 24:13-35 Mk 16:12-13
24. HIS HANDS & HIS FEET — Luke 24:35-45 Mark 16:14
25. UPPER ROOM — John 20:19-23
26. THOMAS on the EIGHTH DAY — John 20:24-29
27. REPORT of the GUARDS — Matthew 28:11-15
28. APPEARANCE to SEVEN in GALILEE — John 21:1-14
29. BREAKFAST LOVE QUESTION — John 21:15-19
30. COMMISSION — Matthew 28:16-20
31. ASCENSION — Luke 24:46-53 Mark 16:14-20

31 days of the HOLY SPIRIT

1. The SPIRIT WILL REST on HIM — Isaiah 11:1-5
2. The SPIRIT of the LORD — Isaiah 61:1-2a,10-11
3. SPIRIT of the SON of GOD — Galatians 4:3-7 & 5:16,22-23,25
4. The BEGOTTEN of the SPIRIT — Matthew 1:18-25
5. HE WILL BAPTIZE YOU in the SPIRIT — Mark 1:1-8
6. BEHELD the SPIRIT — John 1:29,32-34
7. LED by the SPIRIT into the DESERT — Mark 1:12-13
8. BLASPHEMING against the HOLY SPIRIT — Mark 3:22-30 Matthew 12:24-32 Luke 12:10
9. DAVID and the HOLY SPIRIT — Mark 12:35-37
10. The HOLY SPIRIT SPEAKING — Mark 13:1-11
11. FULL of JOY in the HOLY SPIRIT — Luke 10:17-24
12. HOW MUCH MORE — Luke 11:1-13
13. HE WILL TEACH YOU EVERYTHING — John 14:15-26
14. ASCENSION — Beginning of the Book of Acts 1:1-9
15. From ELEVEN to TWELVE — Acts 1:12-17,21-26
16. PENTECOST — Acts 2:1-4,12-13
17. PETER: WITNESSES — Acts 2:37-39 & 5:30-32
18. STEPHEN, FIRST MARTYR — Acts 7:54-60
19. PHILIP in SAMARIA — Acts 8:5-8,14-20
20. CONVERSION of SAUL — Acts 9:1-9,17-19
21. ANOINTED with the HOLY SPIRIT — Acts 10:37-45
22. FIRST CALLED CHRISTIANS — Acts 11:19-26 & 13:1-4
23. LETTER to the NATIONS — Acts 15:22a,23-29
24. PAUL LAYING HANDS — Acts 19:1-10
25. PAUL to the ELDERS of EPHESUS — Acts 20:22-32
26. PAUL in ROME — End of the Book of Acts 28:25b-31
27. SPIRIT of ADOPTION — Romans 8:14-27
28. JOY in the HOLY SPIRIT — Romans 14:13-19
29. PETER on PROPHECY — 2nd Peter 1:16-21
30. UNITY of the SEVEN ONES — Ephesians 4:3-6
    DO NOT GRIEVE the HOLY SPIRIT — Ephesians 4:25-32
31. By the POWER — Ephesians 3:16-21

appendix a - Into which ANGELS LONG to LOOK — 1st Peter 1:10-12
appendix b - The SPIRIT SEARCHES ALL THINGS — 1st Corinth 2:1-16

31 days on the CHRISTIAN LIFE

1. O the DEPTH — Saint Paul to the Romans 11:30-36
2. CROWD TOO MANY to NUMBER — Saint John in the Book of Revelation 7:9-12
3. COMFORT-ENCOURAGEMENT — Paul in 2nd Corinthians 1:3-7
4. DOING GOOD — Paul, in 2nd Thessalonians 3:7-13
5. PUT ON the LORD JESUS CHRIST — Paul to the Romans 13:11-14
6. CHILDREN of GOD — 1st Letter of Saint John 3:1-3
7. WORD PLANTED in YOU — Letter of Saint James 1:19-27
8. REBIRTH to a LIVING HOPE — 1st Letter of Saint Peter 1:3-9
9. THESE THINGS ABOUNDING — 2nd Letter of Peter 1:3-11
10. GRACE of GOD — Paul to the Colossians 1:3-6
11. CHILDREN of the DAY — Paul in 1st Thessalonians 5:1-11
12. ALL HAVE SINNED — Paul to the Romans 3:21-31
13. I AM PERSUADED — Paul to the Romans 8:35,37-39
14. LIVING and ABIDING WORD of GOD — 1st Ltr of Ptr 1:22-25
15. IF YOUR ENEMY IS HUNGRY — Paul to the Romans 12:9-21
16. GOD IS LOVE — 1st Letter of John 4:15-21
17. MERCY EXULTS over JUDGMENT — James 2:1-13
18. ONE IS the LAWGIVER & JUDGE — James 4:1-12
19. CHARISMS — Paul to the Romans 12:1-8
20. GOOD STEWARDS of GRACE — 1st Letter of Peter 4:7-11
21. SUFFICIENT to YOU IS MY GRACE — 2nd Corinth. 12:1-10
22. To THIS YOU WERE CALLED — 1st Letter of Peter 3:8-11
23. LET ENDURANCE WORK — Letter of James 1:2-11
24. GOD IS the ONE WORKING in YOU — Paul to the Philippians 2:12-16
25. THIS IS MY GOSPEL — Paul in 2nd Timothy 2:1-13
26. For GOOD & for BUILDING UP — Paul to the Romans 15:1-5
27. WALK as HE HIMSELF WALKED — 1st Letter of John 2:1-6
28. PUT ON the NEW HUMAN — Paul to the Colossians 3:5-17
29. BE RECONCILED — Paul to the Colossians 1:21-28
30. CHRIST LIVES in ME — Paul to the Galatians 2:15-21
31. NEW HEAVENS and a NEW EARTH — End of the 2nd Letter of Peter 3:1b-18

CANTICLES

Think of a Canticle as a Poem or a Song that has been inserted into a text, as if you were writing a letter or recording a video for a loved one and included in it their favorite poem or song.

OLD TESTAMENT CANTICLES

Exodus 15:1b-4,8-13,17-18 – Saturday Morning, 356
Deuteronomy 32:1-12 – Saturday Morning, 360
1 Samuel 2:1-10 – Wednesday Morning, 332
1 Chronicles 29:10b-13 – Monday Morning, 317
Tobit 13:1b-8 – Tuesday Morning, 324
Tobit 13:8-11,13-15 – Friday Morning, 352
Judith 16:1,13-15 – Wednesday Morning, 331
Wisdom 9:1-6,9-11 – Saturday Morning, 358
Sirach 36:1-6,13-22 – Monday Morning, 318
Isaiah 2:2-5 – Monday Morning, 316
Isaiah 12:1b-6 – Thursday Morning, 342
Isaiah 26:1b-4,7-9,12 – Tuesday Morning, 323
Isaiah 33:13-16 – Wednesday Morning, 336
Isaiah 38:10-14,17b-20 – Tuesday Morning, 326
Isaiah 40:10-17 – Thursday Morning, 340
Isaiah 42:10-16 – Monday Morning, 320
Isaiah 45:15-25 – Friday Morning, 346
Isaiah 61:10-62:5 – Wednesday Morning, 334
Isaiah 66:7-14a – Thursday Morning, 343
Jeremiah 14:17b-22 – Friday Morning, 348
Jeremiah 31:10-14 – Thursday Morning, 339
Ezekiel 36:24-28 – Saturday Morning, 355
Daniel 3:26-27,29,34-41 – Tuesday Morning, 328
Daniel 3:52-57 – Sunday Morning, 314
Daniel 3:57-90 – Sunday Morning, 312
Habakkuk 3:2-4,13a,15-19 – Friday Morning, 350

NEW TESTAMENT CANTICLES

Luke 1:46-55 – Canticle of Mary: the Magnificat (Morning Prayer), 380
Luke 1:68-79 – Canticle of Zechariah: the Benedictus (Evening Prayer), 378
Luke 2:29-32 – Canticle of Simeon (Night Prayer), 30
Ephesians 1:3-10 – Monday Evenings, 322
Philippians 2:6-11 – Saturday Evenings, 363
Colossians 1:12-20 – Wednesday Evenings, 337
Revelation 4:8b,11; 5:9,10,12,13b – Tuesday Evenings, 330
Revelation 11:17-18; 12:10-12a – Thursday Evenings, 345
Revelation 15:3b-4 – Friday Evenings, 354
Revelation 19:1b,2a,5b,6b,7 – Sunday Evenings, 315

SAYINGS OF JESUS & OTHER ANTIPHONS

Be not afraid, 279, 132, 165

Matthew 1:21, 46 Matthew 1:23, 25 Matthew 2:6, 140 Matthew 3:17, 56 Matthew 4:19, 52
Matthew 5:3, 8 Matthew 5:4, 88 Matthew 5:5, 302 Matthew 5:6, 230 Matthew 5:7, 292
Matthew 5:8, 27 Matthew 5:9, 316 Matthew 5:10, 152 Matthew 5:11, 290
Matthew 5:13a,14a, 80 Matthew 5:16, 295 Matthew 5:19, 11 Matthew 5:38,39, 136, 242
Matthew 5:40, 13 Matthew 6:6, 212, 245 Matthew 6:24b,21, 99 Matthew 6:26, 271
Matthew 6:34, 120 Matthew 7:1, 117 Matthew 7:24, 60 Matthew 8:15, 190
Matthew 8:17, 145 Matthew 9:12,13b, 246 Matthew 9:13a, 12:7, 101 Matthew 10:6, 201
Matthew 10:28, 133 Matthew 10:37, 176 Matthew 10:38, 180 Matthew 10:39, 268
Matthew 11:28,30, 119 Matthew 13:16,17a, 72 Matthew 13:23, 124 Matthew 13:30, 171
Matthew 13:33, 89 Matthew 13:45,46, 116 Matthew 13:52, 255 Matthew 14:27,29, 169
Matthew 14:31, 229 Matthew 16:26, 280 Matthew 18:20, 192 Matthew 18:22, 233
Matthew 18:35, 207 Matthew 21:31, 50 Matthew 21:43, 162 Matthew 22:21, 194
Matthew 22:37,39, 32 Matthew 23:3b,4, 275 Matthew 25:13, 122 Matthew 25:29, 272
Matthew 25:35,36, 45 Matthew 28:20, 96

Mark 1:3, 340 Mark 1:15, 48 Mark 2:9-11, 84 Mark 2:15, 41 Mark 2:22, 21
Mark 2:27, 164 Mark 2:28, 150 Mark 3:5, 350 Mark 3:25, 78 Mark 3:35, 274
Mark 4:25, 276 Mark 4:26,27, 186 Mark 4:41, 222 Mark 5:30, 58 Mark 5:41, 267
Mark 6:7a, 322 Mark 6:8, 97 Mark 6:31, 244 Mark 7:15, 74 Mark 7:21,22, 77
Mark 8:27,29, 254 Mark 8:31, 236 Mark 9:7, 24 Mark 9:31, 109 Mark 9:37b, 110
Mark 10:15, 108 Mark 10:45, 264 Mark 10:51,52, 270 Mark 12:29, 35
Mark 13:31, 28 Mark 16:15, 296

Luke 1:47, 332 Luke 2:29-32, 30, 213 Luke 2:49, 167\ Luke 2:52, 358 Luke 3:10, 342
Luke 4:4, 184 Luke 4:8, 243 Luke 4:18, 39 Luke 4:24, 137 Luke 4:40b, 106 Luke 5:4, 286
Luke 5:32, 250 Luke 6:20b, 23 Luke 6:23, 92 Luke 6:27, 288 Luke 6:36, 309
Luke 6:38, 251 Luke 6:41, 16 Luke 7:6,7, 238 Luke 7:14, 15 Luke 7:16, 202
Luke 7:44,47, 64 Luke 8:11b, 112 Luke 9:13a, 262 Luke 9:14, 228 Luke 9:16, 312
Luke 9:50, 204 Luke 9:58, 19 Luke 9:60, 174 Luke 10:2, 126 Luke 10:11b, 343
Luke 10:29, 38 Luke 10:37, 37 Luke 11:9, 260 Luke 11:13, 269 Luke 12:15, 182
Luke 12:34, 66 Luke 12:49, 82 Luke 13:30, 259 Luke 14:10,11, 129 Luke 14:33, 142
Luke 15:7, 256 Luke 16:13, 232 Luke 17:17, 199 Luke 18:8, 265 Luke 18:13, 70
Luke 19:5, 298 Luke 19:10, 300 Luke 19:42a, 160 Luke 20:38, 30 Luke 21:15, 198
Luke 23:34, 123 Luke 23:43, 266 Luke 24:46, 12

John 2:7,8, 196 John 3:8, 9 John 3:16, 285 John 3:17, 314 John 3:21, 226 John 3:30, 308
John 4:34, 282 John 5:6, 94 John 6:12, 248 John 6:33, 154 John 6:35, 273 John 6:51a, 304
John 6:51b, 68 John 7:37, 355 John 8:7, 148 John 8:12c, 337 John 10:4, 86 John 10:14, 239
John 10:30, 173 John 12:24, 257 John 12:26b, 104 John 12:32, 258 John 13:14, 237
John 14:23, 234 John 14:26, 247 John 14:27a, 128 John 15:1, 42 John 15:12, 114
John 15:17, 306 John 16:12, 18 John 16:13, 261 John 18:34, 189 John 20:21, 209
John 20:23, 87, 217 John 20:29, 263

Acts 1:21-22, 163 Acts 4:32a, 278 Romans 14:17, 346 2 Corinthians 12:14, 317
1 Timothy 2:2, 55 1 Timothy 2:3b,4, 270 Philippians 2:3, 363 Hebrews 11:29a, 356
James 4:12, 166 1 Peter 3:15b, 249 1 Peter 5:7, 252 1 John 1:8,9, 26 Revelation 1:8, 345
Revelation 4:8b, 330 Revelation 15:3a, 354 Revelation 21:5b, 324 Revelation 21:10,11, 352

Genesis 1:31a, 253 Leviticus 19:18, 32 Deuteronomy 6:5, 32 1 Chronicles 29:14b, 317
Psalm 34, 318 Isaiah 42:6a, 320 Isaiah 43:1-5a, 165 Isaiah 53:4, 145 Isaiah 58:6, 39
Isaiah 61:1-2, 39 Jeremiah 1:5, 348 Jeremiah 7:5b,6, 39 Jeremiah 24:7b, 339
Job 38-42, 341 Hosea 6:6, 101 Micah 5:2, 140 Micah 6:8, 27

CORNER NOTES

A Franciscan Blessing, 221
A Latin American Prayer, 344
A Living Gospel, 34
All Shall Be Well, 333
An Easter Prayer of the Confirmed, 353
Anger the Jesus Way, 351
Apostle, One Who is Sent, 163
A Prayer in Addiction, 201, 278, 321, 355
As a Child Rests in a Mother's Arms, 275
Awareness, 206, 268, 348
Babylonian Exile, 285
Beatitudes, 292
Beloved Son, 24
Be Not Afraid, 132, 279
Big Stories of the Old Testament, 357
Breton Fishing Prayer, 189
Called by Name, 165
Chapter-a-Day Reading Plan, 376
Conscience, 91, 348
Consciousness Examen, 348
Contemplative Life, 10, 103, 197, 212, 315, 355, 364
Culture of Vocations, 127, 297
Debasement, 73
Do Not Judge, 118, 148
Easter makes all the difference, 87, 274, 327
Evangelization, 88
Every Age & Country, 187
Examen of Consciousness, 348
Fear, 93, 132, 165, 279
Franciscan Blessing, 221
Freedom from Addiction, 321
Friendship, 315
Gifts of the Holy Spirit, 353
God Questions, 341
God's Universal Salvific Will, 270
Grace, 307
Gratitude, 121, 272
Hallel Psalms, 241
Hallelujah!, 212, 315
Harmony of Tensions, 65
Humility, 73
Idolatry, 319
Insert Your Name, 165
Intercessions, 378
Intimacy, 335
In Years to Come, 81
Is God the Greatest?, 361
Jesus Prayer, 71
Job Answers, 341
Justice, 39, 344
Lamentations, 147
Lectio Continua, 376

Lectio Divina, 377
LGBTQIA+ Discovery, 41, 91, 193, 271, 347
List, 179
Liturgy of the Hours, 187, 309
Lord's Prayer, 379
Lord Take Me, 283
Mary, Mother of God, 238
Monks, 20, 59, 98, 161
Mountain, 173
My Cross, 181
Mystery, 265, 294
Name of God, 40, 284
Night Prayer, 30, 184
Omitted Psalms, 115, 166, 227
One Adulterer Is There, 148
Our Father, 381
Parable of the Latrine, 77
Paranoia, 17
Parents, 275
Perfection expectations, 36
Personal Vocation, 336
Petitions, 378
Place of Business, 95, 183
Possessions, 144
Praying Deeper, 231
Priest-Prophet-Royal-Lover, 267
Principal & Foundation, 63
Psalm Attributions, 12, 187
Psalm Doesn't Apply to Me, 51
Psalm of the Elders, 139
Religious Freedom, 91
Respect, Compassion & Sensitivity, 271
Restless Heart, 172
Sandwiches, 269
Seeker-Disciple-Minister-Apostle, 267
Servant Songs, 151
Simplicity, 303
Singing, 128, 309, 331
Son of Humanity, 151
Sophia Lady Wisdom, 358
Spirit Breath, 34, 40, 87, 128, 188, 353
Subordinate Caste, 22
Suffering Servant, 151
Take Off your Sandals, 268
The Tricky Part, 14
Vocations, 62, 127, 297
What the Prophet Does, 325
Who Am I to Judge? 347
Who Is My Neighbor? 38
Widows, Orphans & Alien Strangers, 39
You Want to be a Saint, 330
Workers in Offices, Shops & Markets, 95, 183

CORNER QUOTES

James Allison, 193
Herbert Alphonso, S.J., 336
Sister Wendy Beckett, 277
Fr Phillip Breen, 278
Frederick Buechner, 62
Breton Fishers, 189
Will D. Campbell, 235
Catechism of the Catholic Church, 91, 271
Jean-Pierre de Caussade, S.J., 34
Anthony de Mello, SJ, 125, 272, 354
Iris DeMent, 265
Serafine Di Giacomo, 188
Sister Ruth Fox, OSB, 221
Pope Francis, 41, 65, 347
Mahatma Gandhi, 136
Gerard Goggins, 201
Sister Thelma Hall, R.C., 268
Hasidic saying, 57
Mychal Judge, OFM, 283
Julian of Norwich, 333
Thomas Keating, OCSO, 355
Peter Keese, 59
Soren Kierkegaard, 294
Jonathan Larson, 109
Mark Link, S.J., 348
Gabriel Marcel, 115
Thomas Merton, 8, 10, 121, 197, 330, 359
Martin Moran, 14

James Martin, S.J., 55, 271
D.T. Niles, 88
Henri Nouwen, 36
Evagrius Ponticus, 20, 103, 314
John Jacob Raub, 67
Sister Helen Prejean, 307
Saint Anthony of Egypt, 98, 314
Saint Augustine of Hippo, 172, 315, 331
Saint Benedict of Nursia, 59
Saint Francis of Assisi, 59, 144
Saint Gregory Nazianzen, 128
Saint Ignatius of Loyola, 59, 63, 348
Saint Irenaeus, 274
Saint John Chrysostum, 303
Saint John the Baptist, 342
Saint Paul of Tarsus, 317
Saint Pope Paul VI, 195
Saint Teresa of Avila, 329
Saint Teresa of Kolkata, 85
Maria Sktodowska-Curie, 93
Mark E, Thibodeaux, S.J., 231
James Thurber, 206
Paul Wachdorf, 6, 377
Benedicta Ward, 161
Isabel Wilkerson, 22
Greg Wolf, 179
Anthony Zoghby, 262

IMAGES
by Stephen Joseph Wolf

Alleluia, 28
Anger the Jesus Way, 106
Away from the Cross, 113
Baptism of the Lord, 56
Cosmology of the Ancients, 310
Crucifixion, 290
Footwasher, 338
Hildegard Mandala, 170

Holy Family, 54
Jesus on the Cross, 202
Light of Christ, 200
Mother of Tenderness, 362
Nativity, 46
Nativiy Cross, 227
Unity in the Trinity, 287
Unity Cross, 188

One Chapter-A-Day, to read the whole Bible in 44 months in *Lectio Continua*

One plan: Begin with the shortest Book (2nd John with 13 Verses) and read through to the longest (Isaiah with 66 chapters). Don't skip the footnotes!

PENTATEUCH
- 50 Genesis
- 40 Exodus
- 27 Leviticus
- 36 Numbers
- 34 Deuteronomy

HISTORICAL
- 24 Joshua
- 21 Judges
- 4 Ruth
- 31 1st Samuel
- 24 2nd Samuel
- 22 1st Kings
- 25 2nd Kings
- 29 1st Chronicles
- 36 2nd Chronicles
- 10 Ezra
- 13 Nehemiah
- 14 Tobit
- 16 Judith
- 10 Esther
- 16 1st Maccabees
- 15 2nd Maccabees

WISDOM BOOKS
- 42 Job
- 41 Psalms 1-41
- 31 Psalms 42-72
- 17 Psalms 73-89
- 17 Psalms 90-106
- 44 Psalms 107-150
- 31 Proverbs
- 12 Ecclesiastes
- 8 Song of Songs
- 19 Wisdom
- 51 Sirach

THE PROPHETS
- 66 Isaiah
- 52 Jeremiah
- 5 Lamentations
- 6 Baruch
- 48 Ezekiel
- 14 Daniel
- 14 Hosea
- 4 Joel
- 9 Amos
- 21 vs. Obadiah
- 4 Jonah
- 7 Micah
- 3 Nahum
- 3 Habakkuk
- 3 Zephaniah
- 2 Haggai
- 14 Zechariah
- 3 Malachi

THE GOSPELS
- 28 Matthew
- 16 Mark
- 24 Luke
- 21 John
- 28 Acts

PAULINE LETTERS
- 16 Romans
- 16 1st Corin.
- 13 2nd Corin.
- 6 Galatians
- 6 Ephesians
- 4 Philippians
- 4 Colossians
- 5 1st Thess.
- 3 2nd Thess.
- 6 1st Timothy
- 4 2nd Timothy
- 3 Titus
- 23 vs. Philemon
- 13 Hebrews

CATHOLIC LETTERS
- 5 James
- 5 1st Peter
- 3 2nd Peter
- 5 1st John
- 13 vs. 2nd John
- 15 vs. 3rd John
- 25 vs. Jude
- 22 Revelation

LECTIO DIVINA
lek'-see-oh div-ee'-nuh

1. *Lectio* – Read the passage of the word of God with attention, silently, aloud, or in a whisper. If drawn to a word or phrase or image, stop.

2. *Meditatio* – Breathe. Repeat the word or phrase or image over and over as you breathe. Let it sink into your mind, heart, soul and strength. Savor the word. Ask just one question: *Why this? What do you wish to say, Lord?*

3. *Oratio* – Be not afraid to enter into a spontaneous and loving dialogue with God. Talk to God as you would talk to your closest most intimate friend. Be totally honest about what you are thinking and feeling. Are any memories provoked? What do you want to say to God who loves you just the way you are? You may be drawn to praise, thanksgiving, contrition, petition, desires, decisions, resolutions, commitments, dedications… God is interested in everything you have to say and will not judge you. You get to decide whether you will integrate this Word of God into your heart, life and work, or whether you will reject it or dismiss it as of no worth or value to you.

4. *Contemplatio* – For the remainder of the time you have set aside, go back to the word, phrase or image. Breathe. Relax. Simply repeat the word, phrase or image over and over. When distracting thoughts or feelings enter your mind (they will), go back to your word. There is nothing to accomplish; just give this time to the God who loves you. Sitting in God's presence in this silence, you are making an act of faith that God is working in you in God's own time and way. When your time is up, offer a prayer of gratitude. Many people who do *Lectio Divina* find regular journaling helpful.

CANTICLE of ZECHARIAH (The Benedictus)
LUKE 1:68-79

+ **Blessed be** the Lord the God of Israel
who chose a people to visit with redemption,
and raised salvation in the house of David,
saving strength from God's own servant,

speaking from the age of the prophets
through the mouth of the holy prophet:
Salvation out of enmity,
even out of those who hate us,

to show our ancestors how mercy works, -
and to remember the holy promise of the Lord,
the covenant made for our ancestor Abraham,
calming our fear and making us free
to serve with holy justice before God all our days.

And you also child -
will be called a prophet of the Most High
for you will go before the Lord to prepare his way
and give to people a knowledge of salvation
known in accepting forgiveness of their sins.

From the tender mercy of our God,
the sun rising from the height will visit with light
for those who sit in the dark or shadow of death
and to guide our feet into the way of peace.

•

RAINBOW PSALMS IN 30 DAYS

PETITIONS FOR THE CONSECRATION TO GOD
OF THE DAY AND ITS WORK

- For all peoples of faith doing good in the world...
- For secular authorities and all serving as stewards...
- For people who are poor or sick or in sorrow...
- For the basic needs of each human being...
- For awareness of being created in the image of God...
- For discovery and discernment of our charisms...
- For consensus on both rights and responsibilities...
- For loving respect for folks who think differently...
- For God's healing of the core wounds of enemies...
- For the world peace that only God can give...
- For elders who feel abandoned...
- For just treatment of migrant workers and refugees...
- For the starving child awakening our conscience...
- For those suffering physical and mental torture...
- For people living in subhuman conditions...
- For human beings enslaved or unjustly imprisoned...
- For workers in degrading or unsafe conditions...
- For laborers where treated as mere tools for profit...
- For rejection of judging the inner guilt of others...
- For a culture of vocations all over the world...
- For those who have asked for my prayer...
- For those for whom I have promised to pray...
- For those who weigh on my heart...

THE LORD'S PRAYER

• • •

CANTICLE of MARY (The Magnificat)
LUKE 1:46-55

+ **My soul** is stretched full with praise of the Lord,
and my spirit, beyond joy in God, my Savior,
who chose to lay eyes on this humble servant.

Behold, now and forward,
each and every age will call me blessed,
for the Mighty One did great things to me.

Holy is the name and the mercy
to generations and generations,
the ones fearing the One,

Who scattered the haughty of mind and heart,
pulled the powerful off their high place,
and lifted with dignity the humble in need.

The hungering are filled with good things,
the rich are sent away empty,
and servant Israel is given relief

with a memory of mercy to remember,
the promise spoken to our ancestors,
to Abraham and his descendants forever.

•

INTERCESSIONS

 - In gratitude for blessings…;   Abba, thank you.
 - For the sins of this day…;   Lord Jesus, have mercy.
 - With concerns over tomorrow…;   Holy Spirit, help.

THE LORD'S PRAYER

Our Fath-er, who art in heav-en;
hal-lowed be thy name.
Thy king dom come, thy will be done
on earth as it is in heav-en.
Give us this day our dai-ly bread
and for-give us our tres-pass-es
as we for-give those who tres-pass a-gainst/ us
and lead us not in-to temp-ta/-tion
but de-liv-er us from e\-vil.
A-men.

OR

Our Abba in heaven,
your name be honored
and your reign come
on earth as in heaven.
Give us bread for the day,
forgive us our sins
as we forgive others,
and help us resist
temptation to do the bad
with grace to do the good.
Amen.

• • •

www.ingramcontent.com/pod-product-compliance
Lightning Source LLC
LaVergne TN
LVHW010231240625
814536LV00008B/268